The Lord's Question

The Lord's Question

Thoughts on the Life of Response

Dennis Greyson

Second Edition Copyright © 2001
First printing 2001
Second printing 2011

©1985

First printing April 1985
Second printing 1992

The first edition of this book was funded and published by
The Keter Foundation

ISBN-13: 978-1466309111
ISBN-10: 1466309113
Library of Congress Catalog Card Number 85-50505

Printed and distributed in the United States of America by CreateSpace

Contents

PREFACE

In sharing the following thoughts with others I claim no authority to instruct but only, perhaps, to remind; for the questions I have pondered are addressed to us all.

I the Lord ask you this question . . .

Doctrine and Covenants 50:13

ACKNOWLEDGMENTS

In this second printing of the second edition I want to thank several people. Dennis Packard and James Faulconer created the Keter Foundation, and others gave generous contributions to finance Keter's projects; one of these was the first edition of *The Lord's Question*, which was designed by Thomas Hinckley. Over the years since, Elder Jeffrey R. Holland, Gary Gillespie, Barbara and Cody Carter, Dianne Higginson Seckler, Terry Warner, Cole Durham, John Durham Peters, Tony Kimball, Phillip Hadfield, Randall and Melissa Bradford, Jennifer Goodman, Ann Huefner, Col. John Mark Mattox, Brian Harrison, Charlene Scowcroft, Linda Brummett, Bruce Jorgensen, Ann Madsen, Chris Packard, Debbi Burklund, Lance and Karen Packer, Rick Taylor, Robert Crawford, Karen Greyson, and others have given encouragement in various ways. Linda Hunter Adams, CJ Obray, and Jeanette Call Anderson provided the editorial expertise for producing this edition. My three daughters – Arwen, Rachel, and Mary – have offered unfailing love and support. Three men have shaped my sentiments so profoundly that I honor them as the fathers of my faith: my uncle, John Major Scowcroft; my mission president, Truman G. Madsen; and my Institute teacher, Elder Marion D. Hanks. Finally, a number of readers and reviewers, some known to me and some not, have taken time to share their kindly thoughts.

Since retiring from BYU, I took back the name given to me at birth, the name of my own father, Carl Greyson; I trust that this change will leave no one perplexed.

I

Where Art Thou?

What is a question? I must use one even to ask. Perhaps it is impossible to define something so basic to thought. A question is unique. Yet my life from childhood to maturity has been filled with questions. Wisdom, I have heard, is as much a matter of knowing the important questions as of having their answers. Questions focus my attention and my efforts. They are a summons to learning. Long ago the great teachers found that people learn best when they are asked instead of simply told. A question is a challenge, the beginning of a quest.

There is an old tradition that views man as the being who asks questions. In the words of Aristotle, "All men by nature desire to know." From this point of view man is distinguished by his power to discover. The mark of man is a question. The history of the ages is the record of man's questions. When an old question is answered or even just abandoned and a new one replaces it, then a new age begins. All the knowledge that creates civilization emerges in answer to human questions. The history of religion follows this same pattern, as it tells of man's quest for God. In all things man's progress is the progress of man's questions. They lead to knowledge, and knowledge is power.

There is another tradition even older that makes a different claim. It asserts that man is born into the world with a question and that he lives his life with a question, but it is not man's question. In this view man is not primarily a being who questions, but a being who is questioned. The question addressed to man persists, harder than stone, softer than snow, more insistent than the warmth of the sun. "Where art thou?" (Genesis 3:9.) Man is distinguished not by his power to ask but by his power to hear. The question with which he lives is not his own, but God's.

For all that it has helped man learn, the claim that man is primarily a being who questions is inadequate. It may create minds without hearts. It may lead to the worship of information on the one hand or to skepticism on the other. Even worse, it may lead to despair, for knowledge alone can never satisfy. Will man be happy when he has split the last atom and searched all the sands of the sea? Deeper than the desire to know is the desire to be known. Man's fundamental need is not to ask a question but to respond to one. Only by responding do I learn to be responsible; only by responding do I learn to care about something beyond myself.

The highest task that man can have and the only one that can bring him happiness is to respond to the Lord's question. When I left the Lord to enter mortality, I found his question waiting, and when I leave mortality to return to him, he will meet me with a question. When Adam left Eden, the Lord clothed his body with a garment and his soul with a question. Adam, where art thou? Does God not know? On the contrary, only he knows. In my weakness I lose my bearings. Like a child wandering in a forest I follow the whims of the moment and forget the way. I am too caught up by my surroundings to follow the path. Not until a Father's voice calls do I wonder where I am. How shall I answer? I am here? But where is here? So helpless am I that I cannot say. But deep within I hear his voice and tremble, for finally there are just two places, with him or without him, and just two ways, toward him or not toward him.

The Lord's question gives to man not only a task but an honor, the honor of conversing with God. All the world is God's creation, but only man is God's own child. Only man is made in God's image. The heavenly bodies together with the earth and all its creatures display in their various ways the glory of God. Yet none but man receives his question. To him alone God says, "Gird up now thy loins like a man; for I will demand of thee, and answer thou me." (Job 38:3.)

With a question God gives the gift of choice. He asks; man must respond. To complete his work God Omnipotent seeks for help. Will man choose to give it? All is within the power of God except the love for God. This love for him is within man's power alone. Will man through his choosing finish the work that God through his choosing began? Will man freely respond, freely return? God asks, then God waits. History is not the succession of man's questions. History is the repetition of God's question. Ignored, forgotten, defied, the Divine Patience tarries and watches for the chance to ask once more. "And therefore will the Lord wait, that he may be gracious unto you, and therefore will he be exalted, that he may have mercy upon you." (Isaiah 30:18.) In mercy God repeats his question.

Man, however, still craves at times to question. He may take the myth of Prometheus for a guide; he may call God absolute power and play the role of rebel. How much man loves to play a role! But the wise call God good. As Plato said, "He was good, and the good can

5

never have any jealousy of anything. And being free from jealousy, he desired that all things should be as like himself as they could be." Man cannot rob heaven, not because God will defend it, but because He has already offered it to man. Man's concern was first God's concern. Still sometimes I wonder, why is injustice permitted to endure? How can heaven allow such suffering? What is the purpose behind that? I see friends whose faith fails. Why?

My questions—how important they seem. And yet I ask no question that I have not learned from God. If with Abraham I demand, "Shall not the Judge of all the earth do right?" (Genesis 18:25), I must not forget that he taught me what is right. My love for goodness is a mirror of his own. My longing for justice is deep because he is my Father. My concern for others is full because he is their Father too. Made in his image, all men show forth his nature, and all their questions finally come from him and lead to him. "Wherefore, I the Lord ask you this question—unto what were ye ordained?" (Doctrine and Covenants 50:13.) All man's beginnings and endings occur within the circle of these words. Man was ordained to disclose the Divine; his work is to become like God. The trials of life are the way of perfection. Whatever doubts or defeats, insults or desertions, whatever perplexities I must face, whatever grief I must endure, I cannot go where God has not been before. When man the questioner hurls to heaven his cry of loneliness, he only repeats the Lord's question, "My God, my God, why hast thou forsaken me?" (Mark 15:34.)

God gives his question before he gives his answer so that I may learn to understand the answer. Each step of a staircase supports my ascent only after I have first raised my foot to a higher level. God's question calls me to a higher level of living. When I have reached it, I will find his answer at the same time, firmly supporting me. Even the commandments may be viewed as questions, although they are not phrased as such. They are questions addressed to faith. "And we will prove them herewith, to see if they will do all things whatsoever the Lord their God shall command them." (Abraham 3:25.) God commands the other parts of his creation besides man. But his commandments to the stars and seasons, the days and nights, the winds and the tides are not questions. They are not questions because these things are not free.

The commandments given to man may be viewed as questions because man is free. Man's response of obedience is the free response of love. I obey not because I must but because I will. The Lord wants me, even me, to be his companion. "Can two walk together, except they be agreed?" (Amos 3:3.) As I hearken and obey, as I quickly respond, I show my desire to be in agreement with him. But do I always respond quickly? Do I always recognize him? What of the stranger from Emmaus? What of the poor wayfaring man of grief? How long do I take to answer? How often do I waver in my steps? Have I sometimes seen him and passed by on the other side? These questions too are his questions, reminding me that more than words are needed to answer him.

To most questions man wants to have an answer. But to the Lord's question man must *be* an answer. From man, God does not need information. Man's response must be man's own self. As each human being is different, so will be each response. None is unnecessary, none without worth. Once a man named Zusia taught this lesson. When, he said, the Lord calls me to be judged, perhaps he will ask, "Zusia, why were you not like my servant Abraham?" And I will answer, "Lord, Abraham was the father of nations, the receiver of thy great promises. But I am only Zusia." Perhaps he will ask, "Zusia, why were you not like my servant Moses?" And I will say, "Lord, thy servant Moses led thy people from Egypt; he received thy law upon the mount. But I am only Zusia." But what shall I answer when he asks, "Zusia, why were you not like my servant Zusia?" Man must answer the Lord with man's own unique self.

To be a child of God is to share his divine nature. But that nature is still potential in man, and the purpose of life is to make it actual. Freedom is part of the divine nature, and so freedom is given to man. By his own choices man can become his own potential self. God knows that self already. To guide but not to compel man toward his own true self, God asks his question. As man responds with love, he becomes the self that God knows and wants him to be. Man has invented many names for himself; most of them are wrong. But man wears them like labels and often comes to believe them. Who has not worn with shame and mute belief the name of Stupid or Awkward or Nobody or even Wicked? But God calls to man with a new name that only God can speak. He addresses his children born in his image and asks, "Can you look up, having the image of God engraven upon your countenances?" (Alma 5:19.) Whatever man chooses as his response, he becomes the answer to the Lord's question. How painful it sometimes is to have the wrong answer. How much more painful then to be the wrong answer.

The prophets speak of a last judgment, but that is not the first judgment. Not only then must I answer but now. Often when caught unawares by a question, I respond as if by reflex that I did not hear it. I really did hear, but in a bid for more time I ask that the question be repeated. The Lord does not try to catch me unawares. He repeats his question. A thousand times in a thousand places the Lord asks. Just as often I answer. But what do I answer? What self am I building?

All religious people believe that the Creator is concerned about man, but the nearness of his concern may be overlooked. Because of the weakness of man's mind, because of his inability to discern and remember many individual things, man uses abstract ideas to help him. Man speaks of nature, society, humanity. The divine mind does not require such ideas. All things are known to God; therefore, not just mankind but each individual human being is God's object of concern. "The very hairs of your head are all numbered." (Matthew 10:30.) Deep in every human heart is the desire to be known and loved just for oneself. But only One can have such love and knowledge. Men group themselves into classes, races, and nations, but the Father calls them as he called their first parents in the Garden, one by one.

The idea of being pursued is sometimes a disturbing one, even a terrifying one. How often do I want just to be left alone, to be secure, to rest? Yet I am pursued. Wherever I go, I am followed. The Lord follows with his question. I have done what I can. He asks, "Canst thou do more?" I have given what I have. He asks, "Canst thou give more?" I am surrounded by darkness. "Canst thou see light?" I am tempted by evil. "Canst thou remember me?" Always if I listen, the still small voice is there. He to whom all hearts are open, and from whom nothing is hidden, stands by me. In his presence, by my every thought and deed I answer him.

A statement can tell only what is or has been. It is fixed, tied to what cannot change. But man faces a future. Freedom points toward possibility. Man is not only what he has been—he is also what he may become. As the child of the Creator, man too may create. Man too may "make all things new." (Revelation 21:5.) The Lord asks his question to tell man not of things past but of things future. He asks man to choose, knowing that every choice is a step and that man is a pilgrim journeying into the future. Beyond all that was or might have been is that which yet may be. To survey the future and to decide what shall come to pass—can man have a greater task? Man has within himself the future of the world. By his choice man makes the future. By a prayer, a deed, a smile, a song, man can change the course of the world.

Sometimes I wish that God would make things clearer. I would trade my faith for certainty and my hope for proof. But then I would also trade my freedom for bondage. Before the world was, God rejected the plan of certain salvation. He chose instead to create the world for freedom. Life is to be built by choices, and choices cannot be made if I know everything from the start. In the perplexities of life I have the chance, if I will, to choose the right. I can resist illusory certainties and follow faith. I can trust the evidence of things not yet seen which are true. (Alma 32:21.) I can, on the other hand, barter my future for a mess of pottage. How many times in the history of the world has that bargain been struck? Freedom is the birthright of every soul, and yet how cheaply some men sell it. Could I ever become a child of Esau?

On a narrow road near Damascus a man named Saul pursued his narrow purpose. Blinded by a sudden light, he fell to the earth and listened: "Saul, Saul, why persecutest thou me?" (Acts 9:4.) Six words undid Saul's purpose. A question remade his life. The Lord's question destroys man's perverted sight and replaces it with a vision of truth. The Lord's question blocks the path of error and removes all worldly comfort. Into man's spiritual shell God places his question like a grain of sand. And man's work, daily renewed, is to make of it a pearl of great price.

The Lord's question is a gift of wisdom and goodness. It comes to me in my time of need, reminding as it teaches, guiding as it coaxes. In moments of doubt it returns to me and answers by asking, "What greater witness can you have than from God?" (Doctrine and Covenants 6:23.) Then I remember how much I have been given and how much I owe. In the Lord's asking is his instruction. In my responding is my redemption.

2

Do Not I Fill Heaven and Earth?

The scriptures do not teach man just a way of life—they teach him life itself. They surround him with the things of God, both visible and invisible. In scripture common things return to their origin and show themselves anew, fresh from the hand of God. Shepherds and sheep, lilies and seeds, water and bread bear cosmic meaning. They display the Divine signature for all who are willing to see. To the skeptic who asks where God is, his creation responds, where is he not? To Moses the Lord said, "And behold, all things have their likeness, and all things are created and made to bear record of me, both things which are temporal, and things which are spiritual." (Moses 6:63.) The beginning of wisdom is wonder, and the object of wonder is the created world.

Some people have supposed and some now suppose that whatever meaning the world contains is found in man's purposes alone. They regard the world as a neutral machine or as an aimless process without purpose or worth. And yet the starry heavens release man's thoughts from merely human things as they lead his mind toward God. Man finds splendor in the morning, majesty in the hills. He takes courage from quiet waters, song from the birds, joy from the flowers. In the beauty of the world around him man finds the words for hymns and prayers.

> Thy mercy, O Lord, is in the heavens; and thy
>   faithfulness reacheth unto the clouds.
> Thy righteousness is like the great mountains;
>   thy judgments are a great deep: O Lord,
>   thou preservest man and beast.

How excellent is thy lovingkindness, O God!
  therefore the children of men put their trust
  under the shadow of thy wings.
They shall be abundantly satisfied with the
  fatness of thy house; and thou shalt make
  them drink of the river of thy pleasures.
For with thee is the fountain of life: in thy light
  shall we see light.
                                        (Psalm 36:5–9.)

How could the Psalmist speak his thankful thoughts without the images of nature? Everywhere he finds evidence for God's goodness. Though much has changed since Adam and Eve walked in Eden, man knows that much has not. The earth is still the Lord's, and as the poet Gerard Manley Hopkins wrote, "The world is charged with the grandeur of God." So strong is the sense that man dwells in a holy place that the prophets instinctively call upon the language of nature. "Sow to yourselves in righteousness, reap in mercy; break up your fallow ground: for it is time to seek the Lord, till he come and rain righteousness upon you." (Hosea 10:12.)

I rise each day to a world of glory, but how often does my mind love its own work more than God's? I build a world of my own, filled with my wants and cares. Within this gloomy cave I choose to live. Enclosed by worry I fail to see the signs of love around me. I miss the chance to make my life joyful and rich. Jesus said, be born again—become as a little child. Was that because the children know the wonder of the world? For them each breath brings new delight. Every color, texture, and sound is a marvel to explore. They look upon the world and find it good. Like Adam in the Garden they see all things as new and beautiful. Their caves are not yet built. Can I leave mine and follow them?

Never shall I lose my memory of one young boy. I see his dark eyes glow with fascination as he watches the furniture being loaded and tied. The truck stands near an apartment building in the gray dirt and litter of a street in the heart of an eastern city. The owners of the furniture are leaving. Soon they will live in a house of their own surrounded by green lawn and flowers. The boy wonders where they are going. He has never heard of Utah. He turns and gazes up the wall of the apartment building. His eyes rest for a moment upon a high windowsill where a row of geraniums is growing. Then they return to the man standing beside the truck. "Will you have a nice apartment? Will you have a garden?" I know at once that this question will follow me forever. Will I have a garden?

The work of man can never be happy until it is joined to the work of God. And of His work "he left not himself without witness." He "gave us rain from heaven, and fruitful seasons, filling our hearts with food and gladness." (Acts 14:17.) From the work of man at its best I can learn the meaning of beauty, but only from the work of God can I learn the meaning of glory. From God's creation I learn wisdom beyond words. I learn a language of praise and love that quiets my power of speech. I listen to the thoughts of the falling rain, the thanks of robins drinking from puddles, the night poetry of creatures who sing while others sleep. These are his witnesses, reminding me that the world is still

God's garden, and that I am his guest, and that all my deeds are done in his presence. "O Lord, how manifold are thy works! in wisdom hast thou made them all: the earth is full of thy riches." (Psalm 104:24.)

To find the glory of the Lord in his creation is not to indulge in sentimental ecstasy. The writers of scripture knew that the lamb and the lion do not yet lie down together. But this knowledge did not prevent them from finding God even in the world as it is. "The young lions roar after their prey, and seek their meat from God." (Psalm 104:21.) Nevertheless, the teaching that God created the earth and all things that are upon it gives to man a special task in the presence of suffering and pain. These were not found on the earth as God first made it. They came as a result of man's fall. Man's challenge then is to help reverse these consequences in every way he can. As God's steward he must heal rather than hurt, build rather than destroy, love rather than hate all nature and its creatures. "How," asked the Prophet Joseph Smith, "will the serpent ever lose its venom, while the servants of God possess the same disposition, and continue to make war upon it?" Nature is under man's dominion but not for sport. The Father marks every sparrow's fall, and man must pay for every act of cruelty.

Though all the earth is the Lord's, still man speaks of holy places. From Mount Sinai to the Mount of Olives, from the Sacred Grove to the Hill Cumorah, man traces his spiritual journey by reference to places. Associated in memory with sacred moments, these places become sacred themselves. The places remembered by many are few. But how many places are remembered by a few or even by one? Everyone may recall a sacred place and a sacred time when the power of God rested upon her. These are the temples without walls where God meets his children.

I cannot say that God's influence is everywhere and leave it at that. For something that is simply everywhere tends to be nowhere in particular. Because I have found the Lord in particular ways and places, I can find him beyond them. Because I know him, I can search for him. I do not infer the living God from nature as a scientist infers gravity from the tides. Although God's influence is everywhere, his Spirit guides me according to my faith and in response to my need. Personal moments of inspiration remind me that my helper is not a principle but a Father. What I love in the beauty of nature points always beyond itself, not just to order or harmony but to him.

At unforgettable times and places the Lord speaks my name. Though his word may not call me beyond the tasks I have already begun, it confirms and purifies their meaning. Any place may become holy and any honest effort may become service to God. The teaching of the scriptures is that I can never know where I will encounter the burning bush or the voice of perfect stillness. I must be always ready to respond. "Do not I fill heaven and earth?" (Jeremiah 23:24.) Wherever I am, God is nigh.

The Lord's question is not only a comfort to the forsaken; it is a warning to the wicked. There are no secret deeds, no hidden schemes. All whispers are heard, all lies discovered, all curses recorded. He permits the tares to grow with the wheat for a season, but the time of threshing will come when the grain will be gathered and the chaff will be burned. The devil has no deeper deceit than the claim that no one will ever know. The all-seeing eye penetrates the darkest shadows. Did God make the moon and stars to remind man that God's light is always present? For those who greet that light with gladness, its name is always love.

> Master of the Universe,
> I will sing a song to Thee.
> Where will I find Thee?
> And where will I not find Thee?
> Where I go, there art Thou,
> Where I stay, there art Thou.
> Only Thou, Thou alone,
> Thou again, and only Thou.
>
> When things go well—Thou,
> And, alas, when things go ill—Thou.
> Thou art,
> Thou wast,
> Thou wilt be.
> Thou reignest,
> Thou didst reign,
> Thou wilt reign.
>
> In heaven art Thou,
> On earth art Thou,
> Above art Thou,
> Below art Thou.
> Where I turn
> And where I stir
> Thou,
> Thou,
> Thou.

This song of Rabbi Levi Yitzhak of Berditchev speaks the prayer I must always utter and the faith I must always seek. I do not love God because he offers me gifts; I love the gifts because they come from God. His presence is his greatest gift. And as I seek him, I know that he seeks me. Whatever else man may be, he is not alone.

It is occasionally said that man is naturally self-interested. But most men do not pursue their own interest. Instead they follow illusions, momentary desires, mutually conflicting wants. They are directed by whim rather than purpose and seek pleasure rather than perfection. The paradox is that man never gains control over his own mind and will until he surrenders them to something higher than himself. The beginning of true self-interest is self-forgetfulness, and the source of real freedom is humility before another. Only the disciple can learn discipline. Jesus has many admirers but few disciples. And yet the Father sent his Son to call all men to follow him. Christ's life alone can give to man the higher pattern that he needs. Reaching all the scattered aspects of man's being, Christ gathers them into wholeness.

If no one else addresses man's hidden longing, He does. If no human voice calls man to surpass his weakness, His does. From Him man receives a task worthy of his labor, sacrifice, and love. And with the task man receives a promise. "Take my yoke upon you, and learn of me; for I am meek and lowly in heart: and ye shall find rest unto your souls. For my yoke is easy, and my burden is light." (Matthew 11:29–30.)

In accepting the Lord's commandments and dedicating my life to his work, I find the meaning of my struggle and the center of my joy. I learn that they are not mine alone but also his, that I am his, and that he will never fail me. And if I am his, he is mine, now and always my guide, my rescue, my "first, fast, last friend."

3

What Mean
the Testimonies?

In the sixth chapter of Deuteronomy these words are recorded: "And when thy son asketh thee in time to come, saying, What mean the testimonies, and the statutes, and the judgments, which the Lord our God hath commanded you? Then thou shalt say unto thy son, We were Pharaoh's bondmen in Egypt; and the Lord brought us out of Egypt with a mighty hand." (Deuteronomy 6:20–21.) Scripture abounds with tales of journeys. The life of man became a journey when Adam and Eve departed from Eden. All men are "strangers and pilgrims on the earth," seeking a far and better place. (Hebrews 11:13.) Though man travels throughout his days, he need not wander. The way is marked by the testimonies of those who have gone before. In scripture the words of prophets whose lives belong to the past guide man's steps as he enters the future.

The testimonies of the prophets leave to others the task of teaching about the world of common experience. Man's natural curiosity is sufficient for his science. The teaching of the prophets comes from beyond the world, and it appeals not to science but to conscience. To hear this teaching is to be blessed but also directed—to interpret, to understand, to teach, and to obey. Those who follow the prophets take upon themselves the task of building the words of scripture into structures of life and then sharing the words with all others.

What mean the testimonies? The question must endure as long as the world, for their full meaning is never-ending. And yet they were given, says the Lord, "unto my servants in their weakness, after the manner of

their language, that they might come to understanding."
(Doctrine and Covenants 1:24.) The words of the prophets direct my deeds and nourish my soul. I will never
exhaust their significance; familiar passages can forever
teach me new things. As the prophet Elijah blessed the
widow's barrel of meal and cruse of oil, so the Lord
blesses the words of his prophets. They waste not, neither
do they fail. Each time I return to them I find a new
portion. (See 1 Kings 17:14.)

To say that the meaning of the revelations is in-
exhaustible is not to say that they are hard to understand. The prophets speak sometimes with figurative
language but their purpose is to teach all men. Their
mission is to declare with plainness the path of the
Lord. World history includes religions of secret doctrines and hidden mysteries, religions in which the
highest teachings were kept from the many and reserved
for the few. But the religion of the prophets is for all.
"The word is very nigh unto thee, in thy mouth, and in
thy heart, that thou mayest do it." (Deuteronomy 30:14.)

How long has it been since I learned something by
heart? What does it mean to know something by heart?
Modern man reads silently and quickly. He corrects his
children from moving their lips when they read. He
tends to confront written words with his eye alone. But
the ancients read aloud. When the disciple Philip was
led by the Spirit to the chariot of the Ethiopian slave,
he *heard* the man reading the prophet Isaiah. (See
Acts 8:30.) Writing in the fifth century, St. Augustine
records his surprise at the extraordinary practice of
St. Ambrose, who read silently. "When he read, his eyes

scanned the page and his heart explored the meaning, but his voice was silent and his tongue was still." How could this habit be explained? Why did St. Ambrose not read aloud like everyone else? St. Augustine hazards the guess that the aged man read silently because "he needed to spare his voice, which quite easily became hoarse." Those of former times did not hurry when they read the word of God. They did not use only their eyes. They placed the word in their mouths and in their hearts.

The ancients saw, heard, and spoke the holy word, and the living spoken word enters the heart. That is one reason why Plato expressed doubt about the worth of writing. He feared that writing would not help, but hurt the power of memory. He feared also that the written word would have little power to inspire the reader by itself. Paul had the same concern when he taught that "the letter killeth, but the spirit giveth life." (2 Corinthians 3:6.) The words of life do not belong in books. "These words, which I command thee this day, shall be in thine heart: and thou shalt teach them diligently unto thy children, and shalt talk of them when thou sittest in thine house, and when thou walkest by the way, and when thou liest down, and when thou risest up." (Deuteronomy 6:6–7.)

On my lips and in my heart the words of the prophets become my own. "Thy word have I hid in mine heart, that I might not sin against thee. . . . With my lips have I declared all the judgments of thy mouth. I have rejoiced in the way of thy testimonies, as much as in all riches. . . . I will delight myself in thy statutes: I will not forget thy word." (Psalm 119: 11, 13–14, 16.) The Psalmist knows what it means to learn something by heart. He will not forget the word of the Lord, for he knows the inner strength this word gives him. He builds his soul with words.

Who can comprehend the power of sacred words? Who can say what things they teach little children whose ears and tongues are trained by the words of God? My language sets "the limits of my world"; I call things around me by the names I have learned. Fortunate are they who have learned the language that teaches of God, for their world will be filled with his presence. Imagine the events of life when they are interpreted in the words of scripture. "In the beginning God created the heaven and the earth." "God created man in his own image." "Honor thy father and thy mother." "As for me and my house, we will serve the Lord." "To obey is better than to sacrifice, and to hearken than the fat of rams." "Though your sins be as scarlet, they shall be as white as snow." "The Lord gave, and the Lord hath taken away; blessed be the name of the Lord." "He that keepeth Israel shall neither slumber nor sleep." "Blessed are the pure in heart: for they shall see God." "Love one another, as I have loved you." "Go ye into all the world." "Feed my sheep." "I am the resurrection, and the life: he that believeth in me, though he were dead, yet shall he live: and whosoever liveth and believeth in me shall never die."

These words give light; no one can see the world aright who does not see it in the light of God. No one can understand the purpose of life who has not found it in the teachings of God. How harsh and empty are the words of temptation in the ears of those who have heard the hymns of heaven!

The testimonies delivered by the prophets summon man to hear and to do. Having heard them, man must choose in the light of their message what he will do. "I have set before you life and death, blessing and cursing: therefore choose life." (Deuteronomy 30:19.) In such circumstances no one would willingly and with eyes wide open choose death. The problem is that man's choices do not always or even often present themselves strictly in terms of life and death, or good and evil. Human existence is much more confused, and most of the time, in order to choose life, man must choose a real good over a merely apparent good. And he must also judge properly the weight of circumstances, for what is good under one set of circumstances—such as the consummation of love within marriage—is not good under a different set of circumstances. Given the inescapable difficulties of choosing wisely, only a fool will ignore the counsels found in sacred testimonies. When man attempts by himself alone to regulate the conduct of his life, he becomes little more than a blind guide. His systems of conduct achieve nothing but a justification of his own weaknesses. How many abuses, for example, has the vague idea of human nature been used to hide? In order to be truly human, man must turn to what is higher than human.

How ironic it is that some of the modern sciences, praised by many as man's highest achievements, have led some of their practitioners to conclude that there is nothing higher than man. And thus having concluded that man is descended from the animals and in the end is nothing more than an animal, they treat him like one. Should one wonder, then, at the fact that many people feel like animals? Instead of the journey to the celestial city there is the modern rat race. The testimony of the prophets is that man, although he shares many things with the other living creatures, has also within his nature a divine spark. He is spiritually akin to God. To him God speaks, to him God sends prophets. In scripture ancient Egypt is the type of a mere animal existence. The prophets call man to leave Egypt and to accept the adventure of righteousness. They do not offer ease but struggle and sacrifice. These are the price of spiritual life and freedom. But for many the apparent security of Egypt seems better than the strenuous liberty of the prophets. A slave can be forced to work but not to grow. Only his own choice can lead him to do this. Nothing prevents man from choosing life and growth except himself. He may stay in Egypt or he may leave. The choice is his.

Despite the difficulties and the effort, those who choose to follow the testimonies of the prophets do not complain but rejoice. In choosing to keep the commandments of God as spoken through the prophets, they choose to do what they were born to do. They thus find their own highest possibility, and in fulfilling it they feel their highest joy. This joy in the Lord is the one thing that skeptics and unbelievers can never understand. From their point of view the law of God is an oppressive weight that is borne by those who are too timid or too deluded to shake it off. But where they see only prohibitions and obscure doctrines, the faithful see truth, enlightenment, and love.

> The law of the Lord is perfect, converting the soul: the testimony of the Lord is sure, making wise the simple.
> The statutes of the Lord are right, rejoicing the heart: the commandment of the Lord is pure, enlightening the eyes.
> The fear of the Lord is clean, enduring for ever: the judgments of the Lord are true and righteous altogether.
> More to be desired are they than gold, yea, than much fine gold: sweeter also than honey and the honeycomb.
> Moreover by them is thy servant warned: and in keeping of them there is great reward.
> (Psalm 19:7–11.)

After the moment of revelation has passed I am to ponder the recorded words. My study is not primarily an act of the intellect alone, and it is not undertaken just to acquire information. My study is an act of worship in which I seek to turn my whole self toward God. In the phrase of the Book of Common Prayer, I am to "read, mark, learn, and inwardly digest" the words of life. Assailed by temptation or just by aimless busyness, I may keep my soul serene by turning to the scriptures. From these, the sacred four, I may draw the strength and the insight to guide me on my way.

The power to speak, to write, to read is precious. Which of the great ones of antiquity could have guessed that long after their palaces and monuments had fallen to dust and ruin, the words of the prophets they ridiculed would still survive? What is a word? A vocalized breath? A set of symbols on paper? Both of these and yet more. *Word* is one of the titles of God himself, the very Son of God who was with the Father at the creation. (See John 1:1.) A word is the sign of intelligence, and intelligence is the glory of God. (See Doctrine and Covenants 93:36.) Man can use words because he is the child of God.

Without the power of words to preserve it, the moment of revelation would vanish without a trace. The past would be but a dim recollection in the mind of each individual, having no continuity with anything outside his own experience. There would be no historical past, no memory shared by all men. Among all the creatures on earth, only man can speak, and only man can record his words. An animal is no inheritor of a past. It begins again, like all its predecessors, with nothing but instinct and its own experience.

To man was given the power to gather into words his wisdom and to hand it on to his children. This handing on is tradition, and it makes the continuity of human life possible. It binds the generations together. Scripture is the most important tradition that man can have, and yet how few people make use of it. Instead they read the news. The news is what will be old tomorrow and without interest. Yet it becomes a narcotic that must be taken daily and that yields no lasting satisfaction but only another craving. "Whosoever drinketh of this water shall thirst again: but whosoever drinketh of the water that

I shall give him shall never thirst; but the water that I shall give him shall be in him a well of water springing up into everlasting life." (John 4:13–14.) The words of Christ and his prophets are lifegiving. They alone can give all other words real meaning.

I can easily convince myself that I have no time to study scripture. But the truth remains: I do what I choose to do; I neglect what I choose to neglect. How often is there no time for reading scriptures when there is ample time for sitting before the glassy face of the electronic idol? If my children do not know the Ten Commandments or the Beatitudes of Christ, it is because I have chosen not to teach them. If they do not love the word of God, it is because I have not shown this love. Modern Israel like ancient Israel has given mankind a book. I belong to the people of a book. We are named after a book. Shall I not then study our holy books?

> Blessed is the man that walketh not in the counsel of the ungodly, nor standeth in the way of sinners, nor sitteth in the seat of the scornful.
> But his delight is in the law of the Lord; and in his law doth he meditate day and night.
> (Psalm 1:1–2.)

Deeds of righteousness and holiness of heart must be learned. Nations do not flourish and children do not mature just by following natural instinct. Always there is the need for discipline and correction, for example, practice, and habit. "For the commandment is a lamp; and the law is light; and reproofs of instruction are the way of life." (Proverbs 6:23.) Those of the present should know that in the past the heavens touched the earth, and holy men and women bore testimony of marvelous things.

The Lord ordained in the beginning that his word should be preserved in testimony. "It was human testimony, and human testimony only," that built faith in ages past. "It was the credence they gave to the testimony of their fathers" that led children to the Lord. Sacred books are precious sources of the things of God. Yet the divine word was not given for books alone. "I will put my law in their inward parts, and write it in their hearts." (Jeremiah 31:33.) Finally the word of the Lord is to dwell in human hearts; the meaning of His will is to be found in man's soul. The scriptures are the spiritual manna that sustains man on his journey through the desert. Each day the ration of life must be gathered. Each word offers strength for another step forward.

There never was a time in which people were more surrounded by words than now. Poured forth from loudspeakers and printing presses by the millions, they flood the world with their inescapable presence. But they are not the words of wisdom. They offer

> . . . neither joy, nor love, nor light,
> Nor certitude, nor peace, nor help for pain.

They roar in my ears with a monotonous rhythm; they drone, they scream, they never cease. Always by their noise they seek to hide the word of God. If I would know it, I must learn to hear it beneath the tumult. Was this what Jesus meant when he said, "My sheep hear my voice"? (John 10:27.) If I have come to know that voice through scripture, I will know it when it speaks through living prophets and through the Spirit to my heart.

What mean the testimonies? How shall I know except I hear them; how shall I understand except I ponder them? They are given for the nourishment of my soul. They are the rod of iron that leads to the tree of life. (See 1 Nephi 11:25.)

The Lord intended that I plant his testimonies in my heart and water them with my care. He intended that I labor to preserve and protect them, that I teach my children to love them. He intended that they be the seeds of my thoughts and the subjects of my meditations. He intended that they be my motives in conduct and my guides in judgment. He intended that they be my summons to prayer and my comfort in need. He intended that they lead me to him.

4

Whom Shall I Send?

After all else has been said, true religion is distinguished finally by the divine initiative. Through the ministry of his Spirit and by the teachings of the prophets, God reveals his truth to man. Many of the prophets have told the story of their summons to serve the Lord, but in the words of Isaiah I find myself. In the question he heard I recognize a question that all men must hear and answer.

Isaiah saw a vision of the Lord surrounded by holy angels. It was as if Isaiah had been permitted to see and hear the heavenly council. The Lord spoke: "Whom shall I send, and who will go for us?" (Isaiah 6:8.) What was the nature of the mission being considered? What would the judgment of the council have been? The record is silent. Upon hearing the Lord's question Isaiah could remain a spectator no longer. He answered the Lord, "Here am I; send me."

Did this prophet of the Messiah know that another voice had responded in another council with these same words? (See Abraham 3:27.) Before the world was created, the Father decreed that it would be made for freedom, and even as he saw the need for a redeemer, he asked for a volunteer. How else could the work of freedom be done? Just as important as man's salvation is man's choice of salvation. In mortal life man may choose without compulsion whether or not he will return to the presence of God. Though I fulfill my obedience to him with my deeds, I consecrate it with my love, and love can never be forced. I may decide for myself if I will follow the pattern of my Savior and his prophet. I may decide if I will accept salvation.

It is sometimes supposed that men must organize in order to effect their plans. It is sometimes said of organizations that development must come from the top down. These ideas have their worth, but they lay too little weight on the role of the individual. Strong leadership will always be needed and prized, but it cannot be responsible for all growth. It is not generally responsible for the most important growth. Trees and children do not grow from the top down. Men do not construct buildings from the top down. The growth that counts is based on roots and foundations and organic processes that are hidden from view. What is exposed is less important than what is not. So it is with people. I cannot look to others or to outside circumstances to provide the basis for my work. The vital strength lies within my own will and the grace of God. The most important struggles and achievements in life are not in society, but in the human heart.

I must choose a standard and then follow it. I must train my soul in the concord of obedience. I must temper my desires and bridle my passions before I can hope to become truly free. My most important labor lies within. This kind of inner work is hidden from view. It cannot be done or seen by anyone but me. Yet nothing is more important, not only for me but for society. As British statesman Edmund Burke said: "Society cannot exist unless a controlling power upon will and appetite be placed somewhere, and the less of it there is within, the more there must be without. It is ordained in the eternal constitution of things, that men of intemperate minds cannot be free." Free societies depend upon free

and self-disciplined individuals. And what is the kingdom of God if not the greatest and highest of all free
societies? To enter it man must master himself.

This truth is hard to remember today because the
individual person seems so weak against the political,
social, and economic forces that combine together in the
world. To be only one—even a disciplined one—appears
hopeless. The group dominates. But the group may create in its members an illusion, a mistaken belief that
joining with others can liberate someone from the burdens of decision and responsibility. Men may forget but
they can never escape their God-given agency. Within
every human being is an immortal soul that must someday, by itself, account for all its choices and deeds. The
group, on the other hand, has no soul, but only the
appearance of one: the group has an image. To share
in this image, to be part of the group, good men may
become bad men; well-trained children may turn from
virtue to vice. "They seek not the Lord to establish his
righteousness, but every man walketh in his own way,
and after the image of his own god, whose image is in the
likeness of the world." (Doctrine and Covenants 1:16.)

The living God condemns in modern as well as in
ancient scripture the idolatry of images. "The Lord
seeth not as man seeth; for man looketh on the outward
appearance, but the Lord looketh on the heart."
(1 Samuel 16:7.) God is not deceived by display, and he
does not need publicity. He does not need to impress.
He does not need groups or important persons. He
needs steadfast faithfulness. He needs those who are
willing to die to the world as wheat in his furrows, those

who will serve him in secret. (See John 12:24.) By his own hand he has promised to do mighty deeds when their time arrives. By my hand he would nourish the hungry each day, "succor the weak, lift up the hands which hang down, and strengthen the feeble knees." (Doctrine and Covenants 81:5.)

What I do for honor or attention is never truly my own, since what I want can be given and taken away by another. But what I do from love is mine together with its joy. A mother rejoices as she places warm covers on her sleeping child. Her loving care needs nothing more than this chance to comfort. I may place the warmth of kindness upon a sleeping, shivering soul. People suffer one by one; so also are they served. As I share the sorrow of the brokenhearted and return good for evil, I share the company of my Master. Deep within I know that for this I was born, not for fame but for compassion, not for power but for love.

It is not the multitude that serve and save the world but the righteous remnant that walk humbly before God. For the sake of ten the Lord was willing to spare Sodom, but they could not be found. (See Genesis 18:32.) Zarahemla narrowly escaped the fate of Sodom because of the few who were righteous. "Yea, wo unto this great city of Zarahemla; for behold, it is because of those who are righteous that it is saved. . . . Behold, if it were not for the righteous who are in this great city, behold, I would cause that fire should come down out of heaven and destroy it." (Helaman 13:12–13.)

Today as in the past God withholds his dreadful judgment for the sake of his Saints. The nations are not preserved by armaments and the threat of war, nor by economic power and technology. Before the God who made all things, these things are as reeds in the wind. The destroying angels are kept from their work by the lives of unknown people "who seek not for riches but for wisdom" (Doctrine and Covenants 6:7) and who try each day to serve the Lord.

Who are they in this generation who serve in secret for the good of all? Who are they who are "called to be saints"? (Romans 1:7.) They who find joy in hidden acts of goodness, they who serve God in the kitchen or in the field, they who know that small deeds reveal the holy. Simple people bear the weight of the world. The world thinks otherwise, but the world is wrong. The world will always ask, "Is not this the carpenter's son?" (Matthew 13:55.) The world will always turn its attention to the highly placed, to the well known, to the visibly important. But God loves humility. He honors those who are righteous rather than those who are known for being righteous. The latter, he has said, have their reward. The Lord who gave beauty to the lilies of the field concealed his own beauty. "He hath no form nor comeliness; and when we shall see him, there is no beauty that we should desire him." (Isaiah 53:2.) Candles on a hill cannot give light without the unseen breath of air. Like the invisible air, hidden holiness sustains the life and light of all.

The cities of the world have their own lights, dazzling enough to blot out the stars. Within their artificial day the things of the world appear real, tangible, desirable; the things of heaven seem only a dream. Above the noise of the city the voice of heaven is rarely heard. How many voices has the city of the world? How often in a day, a year, a lifetime does one soul hear its call? Can anyone count the offers he has had to lie, to covet, to hate, to be unchaste? Is it possible to gather into one heap all the temptations and incitements to evil that even one child has faced? Can anyone measure how much has seeped into his soul? Can he?

Evil has no positive worth of its own. It is always a parasite, a terrible absence of goodness that seeks to draw all things that are good into its own emptiness. This emptiness is the real nature of the world in all its guises. The world has nothing to offer; it can only consume and destroy. Its synthetic smiles and frantic entertainment cannot conceal the void within. On the streets at night, around gambling tables, at bars, in airports, in boardrooms, on golf courses—in countless places the world reveals its true poverty, always in the same way. The eyes of the world are glazed, hard, empty. The sparkle is gone, the innocence is gone, the spontaneous excitement in the new moment is gone. Weary but not from service, old but not with wisdom, they scan the space before them. Perhaps there is still one thrill untried. Perhaps things would be better with a new job, a new house, a new husband, a new wife. Where is there to go after you have been around?

That is not the Lord's question but the devil's. It is the rhetorical question of despair, addressing no person, expecting no answer. It is the cry of a soul who is lost. But such a soul is not forgotten. For the sake of these, the lost, the Master came and comes and calls.

Joy of the desolate, Light of the straying,
Hope of the penitent, fadeless and pure!
Here speaks the Comforter, tenderly saying,
"Earth has no sorrow that heaven cannot cure."
(*Hymn 115*)

For the promise of redemption Christ was sent, and
for the same promise he sends his disciples: to be in the
world but not of the world, laboring for souls seeking to
leave the world, souls "who are only kept from the truth
because they know not where to find it." (Doctrine and
Covenants 123:12.) As a disciple of Christ I may perform
at any moment a saving deed. Wherever I am, the world
will be there too, and others will need my help. I can
bear witness to what is beyond the world. I can testify
that God loves every soul. I can be as a little sanctuary
for his Spirit. At home, at work, along my way, I can be
just. In the midst of compromise I can be constant. I can
seek virtue before advancement, endure humiliation
rather than cause it, speak kindly to anger. My task is to
seek to be a Saint in the most telling way: to forget great
feats and to live a common life, performing routine
duties and daily chores, all with the attitude of sanctity.

I cannot deliberately cultivate this attitude. It rests
upon me when I devote my heart to God and my deeds
to the work at hand, sharing the burden of tedium in
what has to be done, rejoicing in the moments of delight
that God will send. I will find holiness not by intro-
spection alone, not merely by dusting inside my soul
each day, but by turning my mind to others. "When ye
are in the service of your fellow beings ye are only in the
service of your God." (Mosiah 2:17.) He is my courteous

Lord, who always asks my aid. Rarely does he raise his voice; I must listen with care to hear him. By humility and prayer, by faith and love, I can find the means to serve him every hour. My daily conversation can be always with him.

Because God loved man, he sent him away. The whole plan of salvation lies hidden in the paradox of these words: away from the heavenly home, away from Eden, away from childhood, always away. For love seeks not its own. It seeks the good of the beloved, and this good can grow only as the beloved grows.

To become like its father, the child must learn to stand alone. Long ago perhaps I too answered, "Here am I; send me," speaking my willingness to be sent wherever the Father chose, accepting by faith his will without asking what it would be, trusting in all things his wisdom and love.

Now that I am here, can I continue to trust? He has promised to provide for my needs and to make of my work what he wants it to be. Though I do not know where I will be sent or what role I will play, I believe that I am not wandering through life. I believe that I am sent—to parents and family, among friends and strangers, through familiar and foreign places. My mission is known to the Father, and he will prepare my way. He will make of me in my absence from him one who is more worthy to return.

5

Fear Ye Not Me?

One of the most striking features of the Bible is its lack of mythology. A *myth* in the original Greek use of the term was a story of the gods. Ancient pagan religions were steeped in such stories. They told where the gods came from, which usually meant that they told what cosmic forces had generated the gods. The stories varied in detail from religion to religion, but the common theme was the multiplicity of gods.

The Bible contains no such stories. It begins with the majestic utterance, "In the beginning God . . ." and ends with "I am Alpha and Omega, the beginning and the end." (See Genesis 1:1 and Revelation 22:13.) It might be said that the entire Bible is a story about God. His purposes are manifested in all things and at all times. There are no tales of his having come from the union of the sea and the sky, no accounts of his overthrowing primordial deities. Where God is, the gods are not. He dominates all things.

Some writers using the theory of cultural evolution as a guide have tried to derive the religion of the Bible from earlier pagan religions. Such efforts to find the higher in the lower are futile. The difference between the God of Israel and the gods of the nations is stark and clear. Even in the biblical stories that are similar to pagan myths, such as the story of the flood, the differences reveal the unique outlook of the biblical writers. The God of the Bible is sovereign and he is moral. Although he has chosen Israel for a special purpose, his power and concern extend to all the nations. Whatever, according to some, the Bible may have borrowed from other traditions, its core and central message can be explained only in its own terms: it was given by revelation.

When viewed against the background of the other religions of antiquity, the main element of the religion revealed to Israel is the absolute authority of God's will. Because he is Lord over his entire creation, no attempt to explain it without reference to his will can be adequate. What the Bible provides, then, is a sense of ultimate purpose in things. The Bible explains the world in terms of a being who framed it in harmony with an aim of his own. Paganism on the other hand held the view that "all things are full of gods." The gods were personifications of what today are called forces of nature. That is why it was so easy for different religions to identify and worship each other's gods; the basic natural forces and phenomena that the gods personified were common to all men. But as parts of the natural world, the gods could not be used to explain the origin of nature as a whole. Only a being who had created the world could do that.

Although the influence of the Bible has guided Western civilization for two thousand years, there are still those who seek to revive the gods of paganism, only now the gods have modern names: not Kronos but Progress; not Aphrodite but Sex; not Apollo but Culture; not Athena but Science. One has only to survey certain aspects of the modern world to see the cults of the gods still preserved. The point is not to condemn the gods as such, but only the worship of the gods.

The testimony of the prophets has always been that the wonders of the world, great as they are, only bear record of the greatness of their creator. For the prophets all paganism is idolatry in the end—the worship of dead and powerless things. So deep is the aversion of the prophets for paganism that they are unwilling to accept a fine distinction sometimes made in its favor. The distinction is between an idol as a thing that is itself worshiped and an idol as merely a tangible symbol of what is worshiped. For the prophets both the tangible symbol and the force of nature or god for which it stands are equally lifeless when compared to the God who created them. The distinction fails because both sides lead to error. Neither the animate nor the inanimate things of nature have life in themselves. Life comes from God. The supreme and living God alone is worthy of worship.

The tendency toward idolatry remains a constant temptation for man. That is why the testimony of the ancient prophets is reaffirmed by the first of the modern prophets.

> They seek not the Lord to establish his righteousness, but every man walketh in his own way, and after the image of his own god, whose image is in the likeness of the world, and whose substance is that of an idol, which waxeth old and shall perish in Babylon, even Babylon the great, which shall fall.
> (Doctrine and Covenants 1:16.)

All false gods are idols and all will wax old and perish. It must not be forgotten that man himself is part of nature and so are his powers. They too can become gods. An ideal can become an idol. Whenever man places something other than God at the summit of his concern, man turns himself into an idolater. It makes no difference what that thing is; if it is not God, it will separate man from God. And if man is not with God, it matters little what he is with instead.

The discoveries and inventions of modern science, for example, have brought about untold benefits in human life. In the field of medicine alone the improvements made in the human condition are beyond description. But these very improvements provide the temptation to idolatry. Surrounded by his own technical success, man may forget his dependence on God. White-frocked scientists and engineers working in their laboratories can become surrogate priests officiating in modern temples of the gods. Such people can become oracles whose authority is beyond question. There is a sober lesson for the present age in the story of Samson. Unless modern man turns to God, he will go on until, blinded by his idolatry, he uses his great powers to pull down destruction upon his own head.

One of the most harmful features of paganism is its devotion to many gods. The result is that, properly speaking, there is no devotion at all. There is only a loose relativism, a shallow equality of values in which nothing is supremely important. The tendency toward this kind of equality reveals itself today in the popular term "life-style." The suggestion is that one's way of life is simply a style no different in kind from that of one's clothes or furniture. One chooses what one likes, what one is comfortable with. Even in religion pagan indifference occurs. "Worship at the church of your choice." Can one imagine Elijah saying that? Does it really make no difference?

The idea that one religion is as good as another and that man is therefore free to choose should not be confused with another idea. This second idea is that man must be free from constraint in matters of religion. Such constraint usually comes from government. No government may dictate man's religion to him. This doctrine, so important to the heritage of true liberty, was not taught by pagan civilizations but by the prophets of Israel. In pagan societies the king was usually himself a god or the son of a god. The religious order was bound inextricably with the political order. The prophets taught that the king has no religious authority. For trying to claim it on one occasion, Saul lost his kingdom. (See 1 Samuel 13:8-14.) But if the king has no such authority, neither do other men. Man does not create true religion in the way that he creates political orders; he receives it together with its authority from God. Revealed religion has never sought to force man's obedience without first degenerating into apostasy itself. At the same time, revealed religion has never pretended that there is no ultimate truth. "Thou shalt have no other gods before me" is the commandment. (Exodus 20:3).

"Every man walketh in his own way, and after the image of his own god." The idolatry of modern man is the result of pride. He has the biblical tradition behind him, but he turns away. Captivated by the inventions and achievements of his own brain, he succumbs to the temptation of self-worship. The nineteenth-century thinkers who proclaimed that God, as well as the gods, is the product of man's imagination supposed that they were liberating man from an ancient delusion. When

they taught that God was dead, they thought that athe-
ism would bring about freedom from myth. But in fact
they were only returning to paganism. They were creat-
ing a new myth for the origin of the gods: the gods were
no longer generated by sea and sky but by man. Declar-
ing the divine throne vacant, they bade man step forward and claim it for himself. But man is never so
pitiful as when overcome by vanity and never so vain as
when pretending divinity. American poet Ezra Pound
spoke to modern man:

> Pull down thy vanity
> Thou art a beaten dog beneath the hail,
> A swollen magpie in a fitful sun,
> Half black half white
> Nor knowst'ou wing from tail
> Pull down thy vanity
>   How mean thy hates
> Fostered in falsity,
>   Pull down thy vanity,
> Rathe to destroy, niggard in charity,
> Pull down thy vanity,
>   I say pull down.

The idol of modern man is within himself, and so
finding it and pulling it down is all the harder. It is a
hidden idol that man erects today. Few people if any
would regard themselves as idolaters, but many are prepared to sacrifice their own happiness and that of others
to serve some idol. It may be called success or fame or
power or any of a hundred other names. All have the
same lifeless substance; all demand victims.

To men who will not pray, will not serve, will not hearken, the Lord speaks his awful question, "Fear ye not me?" (Jeremiah 5:22.) Fear of the Lord is both the beginning of wisdom and the end of vanity. Such fear ought not to be explained away. Perfect goodness is, as English philosopher Joseph Butler wrote, "the natural and just object of the greatest fear to an ill [evil] man. Malice may be appeased or satiated; humor may change, but goodness is a fixed, steady, immovable principle of action." To the degree that man has evil within him, however little, the being who is supremely good will be an object of fear. But just as truly, to the degree that man has goodness in him, however little, the being who is supremely good will be an object of love.

For man in his present state both attitudes are essential. Fear of the Lord dissolves vanity; love of the Lord creates humility. Working together the two attitudes can transform the self. Pride disappears. Its combination of arrogance and ignorance vanishes. The need to impress and to dominate, the hunger for adulation—these are erased. Man finally stands in the presence of God and whispers the wisdom of Solomon, "I am but a little child: I know not how to go out or come in." (1 Kings 3:7.)

There is a suspicion in the minds of some that humility itself is just one more pretense, a pose that may succeed where others fail. No doubt it sometimes is. But humility can be a pretense only when there is some doubt about its fitness. True humility is humility before God. This is always fitting and never a pretense, for God cannot be deceived. There is no point in pretending before God. That is one reason that I must pray often; it keeps me honest. Prayer requires me to put off my disguises and to be what I am. But in confessing what I am before God, I lay the only solid foundation that can be laid for my own improvement. In my awareness of his perfection and my lack of it, I am also aware that he is, nonetheless, aware of me. Whatever I have done, wherever I may be, he knows how to make me better. "Have I any pleasure at all that the wicked should die? saith the Lord God: and not that he should return from his ways, and live?" (Ezekiel 18:23.)

Humility before God is the soul's response to what man tries to name when he speaks of glory. What is the glory of God? The poets have described it in terms of the heavens and the mountains, pillars of fire and of clouds, and the light of a thousand suns. But God himself says something else: "This is my work and my glory—to bring to pass the immortality and eternal life of man." (Moses 1:39.) For the sake of this eternal purpose the living God gives man the teachings of eternal life.

Like a plumb line beside a sagging wall, these teachings offer man a clear and constant standard. Beyond the confusion of paganism, beyond idolatry and vanity, they state a simple task. "Fear God, and keep his commandments: for this is the whole duty of man." (Ecclesiastes 12:13.) Because they are absolute, the teachings of God have no equal. Having no equal, they require no subtle reconciliations. They need no amendments. Man's understanding will always require improvement, but the teachings themselves are clear and straight and true. They measure all thoughts, all deeds, all lives.

Man is always tempted by the thought that he can flee from God. Everyone sometimes plays the role of Jonah. But there is, as the old spiritual declares, no hiding place down here. Man must choose to be what he will be, knowing that he chooses before God. Life offers everyone enough chances to choose, that doublemindedness cannot be maintained. Finally all my choices will fall into a pattern. What will it be? Each day in a hundred ways I am asked to bend, to follow fashion, to adopt a view incompatible with my covenants. Scripture reminds me that the path of the righteous is narrow. Even if it did not, there are plenty of people willing to tell me. There are people willing to tell me what everyone else does. But that makes no difference. How many times must a disciple of Christ be prepared to admit that he has not seen, has not been, has not done? How many times must he be prepared to assert that he will not see, will not be, will not do? How many books and streets and films and magazines and thrills must he avoid to retain his integrity? More than a few.

Can I who am a pilgrim walk through Vanity Fair and say, I buy the truth? Can I choose and choose again to fear the Lord? Every decision is an act of begetting, and someday I must face my children. I cannot know what they will be like, only that they will be mine. In the awareness of this eventual meeting I should conduct my life, so that my posterity will not condemn, but bless me. Then I may present them every one not with shame, but with joy to the Lord.

6

Knowest Thou
the Condescension of God?

At the center of human history stands one event. Man reckons time in terms of it; man's destiny depends on it. Foreseen by ancient prophets and remembered by faithful followers, it is the birth of Christ.

Filled with the Spirit of God, the prophet Nephi beheld in vision a mother and child. As he gazed he pondered a question: "Knowest thou the condescension of God?" (1 Nephi 11:16.) Nephi's words in reply were as profound as the words he had heard: "I know that he loveth his children; nevertheless, I do not know the meaning of all things." Can more than this be said? That God should become a man to live among men, who can fathom, who can explain all that this implies? Truly one would have to know the meaning of all things to grasp fully the meaning of this single thing.

Yet even in the ignorance of all that this event has done and changed and meant, I know as Nephi knew that its deepest meaning is love. In the awareness that this love is unutterable, still I can tell the story, now and forever, and somehow the words glow with sacred fire, warming and guiding me home.

Long ago, when the earth was new, the voice of God proclaimed: "Let us make man in our image, after our likeness." (Genesis 1:26.) Thus the man and the woman went forth to act as God's stewards over all that he had made. They and their children after them were sent to display the image of God throughout the world. But as ages passed, how hard that task became! Though the journey of life brought gladness, it also brought confusion and failure. Weakness sometimes overcame goodness, and error led to grief. Through the generations diligent souls longed to be better than they were, and cried out the prayer of Jeremiah:

> O Lord, I know that the way of man is not in himself; it is not in man that walketh to direct his steps. O Lord, correct me, but with judgment; not in thine anger, lest thou bring me to nothing.
> (Jeremiah 10:23–24.)

For the sake of man a new beginning was needed, a new way for the children of men to learn who they were and how they should live. According to an ancient teaching, the creation of man had only begun in Eden, but it had not ended there. The words pronounced at the birth of Adam foretold another birth. Though Adam and all his descendants had been born in the image of God, one would yet be born in the lineage and full likeness of God. One would someday come who could truly say: "he that hath seen me hath seen the Father." (John 14:9.) In this one, image and likeness, God and man, would be united; the perfect pattern for a holy life would be given. At Christmastime I remember once more the moment when the creation of man was renewed, when the only begotten Son of God became like man, so that man might become like God.

A thousand years before a thousand years ago a holy night descended on the world. In the darkness of Bethlehem the omnipotent God became an impotent baby. The hands that made the world and hung the stars in the sky were now just large enough to grasp a mother's finger. No pillar of fire appeared, but the living tabernacle of God now lay cradled in a manger. From the moment that the infant Jesus gazed up into his mother's eyes, man's imagination was altered forever. The Christmas story reveals in every mother and child a holy mystery. A vision of the pair at Bethlehem hovers like a halo over all mothers and children wherever the Christmas story is remembered, and in the weakness of a newborn child men feel the thrill of something beyond their power to understand.

For the adversary of all that is good, the arrival of the world's rightful King marked the beginning of the end. When the Lord of all the earth appeared, throughout the evil realm a shudder passed as the angel spoke: "For unto you is born this day in the city of David a Saviour, which is Christ the Lord." (Luke 2:11.) The tiny foot that one day would crush the serpent's head was already nestled in the straw.

The Father's likeness had come at last. Did Joseph and Mary wonder, as they watched the little child, about the humble place of his birth? What would be said of a God who came not in glory but in secret, a King who came not to command but to obey? "I came down from heaven," he later said, "not to do mine own will, but the will of him that sent me." (John 6:38.) This was the way of Jesus; this was the way of humility. His way was not to disclose an ideal from afar, but instead to be a servant and companion, a teacher and friend. He began his life in a stable, that no one should ever feel too lowly to approach him. He claimed no earthly title, that nothing should separate him from those he had come to instruct. He lived a common life, he spoke of common things, and "the common people heard him gladly." (Mark 12:37.)

But the marvel of his coming was that nothing could ever again be merely common. When Jesus entered the world, all things were transformed, not because they looked different, but because he was in their midst. He knew their real worth. As an artist takes common colors and blends them into beauty, Christ took common things and raised them up to sanctity. He led men to see, as they never had seen before, the hidden holiness in the world. Leaven and salt, wind and sea, publicans and sinners—all revealed before his eyes their inner goodness. "For God sent not his Son into the world to condemn the world; but that the world through him might be saved." (John 3:17.) He came to heal and to correct, to restore and to redeem every member of the human family and every part of the created world. I can never tell all that the life of Jesus has touched and blessed, but I know that it brought an assurance of the triumph of love. "For God so loved the world, that he gave his only begotten Son, that whosoever believeth in him should not perish, but have everlasting life." (John 3:16.)

To meditate upon the first Christmas is to find the one true source of meaning for human life. Because this Child was born and this life was lived, man's hope need never die. Celebrating Christmas brings to my heart the excitement that filled faithful hearts so long ago. The spirit of Christmas surrounds and thrills me like the lingering fragrances of pine and spruce and fir.

In the vision of a King born in a stable, attended by the animals and visited by the shepherds, I am led to the ever-startling paradoxes that are the essence of the gospel: out of weakness comes strength; out of simplicity, profundity; out of humility, dignity; out of humanity, divinity. I am freed from the judgments and vanities of the world. I see the wisdom of its wise men perish before a deeper truth as three gifts are laid and human wisdom kneels before a little child.

Gazing in my mind's eye at the silent holy family, I learn anew the uselessness of too much talking, too much asserting, too much questioning. In the Christmas miracle I learn to be patient, to be still, to wait upon the Lord. I share the serenity of the young mother Mary, who "kept all these things, and pondered them in her heart." (Luke 2:19.)

The season of Christmas is a time for seeing all that routine too often hides: the night sky, cold and clear, the beauty of winter snow, the silent vigil of untrimmed trees waiting to be decked with green by spring. While nature rests and beneath the snow protects its life within, I can renew with secret prayer my thanks for the miracle of Christmas. I can smile at a stranger and greet my loved ones with gladness.

The meaning of Christmas lies in sharing. Christ came among men to share what he had brought with him from heaven, but also to share what he would find on earth. The gift he brought was eternal life with all its glory; the gift he received was human life with all its struggles. "For we have not an high priest which cannot be touched with the feeling of our infirmities; but was

in all points tempted like as we are, yet without sin."
(Hebrews 4:15.) In him the very Godhead suffered
because of human weakness. But because he lived and
suffered and died, life and suffering and death were
changed. By sharing them he transfigured them, and
made them ministers of perfection. He revealed that
man's greatness is not to be found in dominion over
the will of another but in submission to the will of God.

To hallow my life he taught me to endure sorrow
rather than cause it, to restrain anger rather than heed
it, to bear injustice rather than inflict it. "Resist not evil"
he said in the Sermon on the Mount. (Matthew 5:39.)
Evil multiplies by the response it seeks to provoke, and
when I return evil for evil, I engender corruption myself.
The chain of evil is broken for good when a pure and
loving heart absorbs a hurt and forbears to hurt in
return. The forgiveness of Christ bears no grudge. The
love of Christ allows no offense to endure. The compassion of Christ embraces all things and draws them
toward himself. Deep within every child of God the
Light of Christ resides, guiding, comforting, purifying
the heart that turns to him.

In the wisdom of God the life of man is a series of
cycles. Their rhythm insures that common yet hallowed
things will come and return again until at last I respond
from within, until my heart has become clean and I am
once more as a little child. What among all the things
that passing seasons bring is more precious to me than
Christmas? When do I come so close to children as
when each year I join the little ones in the wonder of
Christmas? In the darkened room around the Christmas

tree I sense that I too am a child, and the peace of my Father's house surrounds my heart.

Caught up in the excitement of traditional activities, I move from one to another until at last, in my chapel and in my home, the moment comes. I see the children before me in the Christmas pageant. Their shining faces transform familiar housecoats and linens into the splendid raiment of angels, kings, and shepherds. I hear the songs of heavenly choruses as I am led in spirit to the side of the Child Christ.

And now that I have come, what gift shall I leave before him? I know, because he has told me, what will gladden his heart: "Love one another; as I have loved you. . . . By this shall all men know that ye are my disciples, if ye have love one to another." (John 13:34–35.) As I bring the gift of love, I shall see the smile of my Lord Jesus Christ.

7

Wherein Have
I Wearied Thee?

God is man's teacher. He seeks to develop goodness, wisdom, charity. He has placed upon himself one limitation: he will not compel man to learn. Man must reach out to receive all that God has to give. Even more, man must reach out to find it. All learning depends finally on the learner. I have always learned best what I wanted to learn; I have learned best when I was ready and eager to learn.

But this very eagerness sometimes can create a problem. In my beginning ignorance I may take the wrong thing for my immediate goal. I may pursue first what must be last. If this happens, my interest, which is so important, will raise a barrier to learning. Impatient to reach the summit, I forget that the foothills come first.

What I want after all is the result. What I tend to notice most in the world around me are results. I see trees, animals, buildings, books, and tables as finished things. They are complete and available for inspection. No effort is needed to observe them. But the meaning of growth, planning, and sustained effort is harder to grasp. These things are so gradual that they often escape notice. Bare trees do not gain their leaves overnight. They come so slowly that I fail to notice. Then I wake up one morning, and all at once it is spring. Like so many men of my time, I lack the insight of the farmer and the craftsman or the mother with child. These understand the slow and steady pace of time. They know by intimate involvement what can come from patient caring and waiting.

There is value in the power to view things with an eye to finished results. It enables man to organize his knowledge of the world in terms of fixed points of reference. Knowledge cannot be based on pure process or change. But the fact remains that things never simply are. They are always changing; one event is born from another and bears within itself yet another. I too am slowly changing, moving toward some distant end.

Results are important but not all-important. It matters not only what I have but how I got it. When I studied mathematics in school, I learned that the correct solution to a problem is nothing but the assured outcome of the correct procedure in solving it. The solution includes the steps that lead to it. If I wish to learn a language, the facility that I seek will be nothing more than the product of all my separate hours of practice. I know these truths, but often I fail to apply them. My earliest moral errors as well as my latest ones are mainly the consequences of attempts to get results in the wrong and usually shorter way. No result of any importance can be achieved immediately. Time makes diamonds dear.

Life offers many chances to choose, and every choice made brings consequences that must be faced. Everyone wants to have happy consequences; they want to succeed. But some forget that success is not a single achievement. As long as life lasts there will be new choices to face and new consequences to consider. Success is always possible but never final. It is something constantly in need of renewal. And for the most part what is quickly gained can be quickly lost. If I want to acquire great success I must also want to perform great labor, for the two cannot be separated. "All things excellent," said the philosopher Spinoza, "are as difficult as they are rare." Experience teaches this truth to every generation, and each soul must decide how much excellence it is willing to have. Dreams alone cannot replace determined effort. That is not to say that success needs no hope. The long years of daily labor must be bound together by an inward trust that with God's help they will yield something far finer than any dream could tell.

As I contemplate a distant goal, I cannot fail to be aware of those who live from day to day, savoring the pleasures of the moment, caring little for the efforts that distant goals demand. No one can escape the knowledge that a choice to fulfill the commandments of God must be made in a world that chooses only to fulfill itself. And always the world asks its questions too. "If you have left Egypt, where is Canaan?" "Do you really like the desert?" Under such conditions I may sometimes envy those who will not share my efforts. With sound reason the last commandment of the ten forbids envy or coveting. All my labor to keep the others will be undone if beneath my observance I maintain a hidden longing to break them and to be like those who ignore them. There is a sense in which all temptation begins with coveting. I want what another has or what I imagine that I could have. Aloud I may call it worthless, but secretly I want it. Then my conscience reproves me. If I listen and turn my attention away and back to my true task, all will be well. But what if I permit my attention to remain fastened on the forbidden thing? Conscience continues to speak and I continue to crave. In such a condition I begin to doubt my own sincerity. I am led to wonder about the reality of my commitments. Then I wonder about the reality of other people's commitments. Are the voices right that call the religious mere hypocrites?

My hesitations increase my perplexity. No longer pressing forward toward the goal, I allow myself to rehearse over and over again the difficulties of my indecision. I may still resist complete abandonment of my quest; I do not wish to succumb to temptation. But my motive is different. No longer do I refuse temptation because my interest is directed to something else, because I am actively seeking another goal. My mind is now turned inward on itself.

I refuse now self-consciously out of a kind of pride. I refuse because I think myself "above" such a thing. Like the fox who calls the grapes he cannot reach sour, I condemn what tempts me and those whose behavior fascinates me. I find that I covet less when I assume the judgment seat. The craving is appeased not by the pleasure of satisfaction but by the pleasure of condemnation. I am not holy, I admit, but surely I am holier than they.

As I am holier, I ought to be happier. Why then are they so happy while I am not? After all, I am (or was) a pilgrim seeking the holy land while they are scoffers and sinners. Why should their lot be better than mine? They appear quite free from inner turmoil. Finally I allow my mind free rein: having forgotten to keep it fixed on my goal, I let it run headlong into a clash of envy and pride. The one fights the other, but both keep me from my task.

Confusion, resentment, and discouragement transform my mind into a heavy longing for rest. Brought to this point by the burden of a commitment, I seek only to be rid of it. The words of the world ring in my ears: "If it feels good, do it." "Do your own thing." "Why fight it?" "You deserve everything you can get." "All these things will I give thee, if thou wilt fall down and worship me." (Matthew 4:9.) But before I lay down my commitment and turn away, another voice speaks. "Wherein have I wearied thee? testify against me." (Micah 6:3.)

The voice offers no arguments and states no defense. It challenges me to speak; it tells me to present my case. As I try to formulate a complaint, the incoherent monologue of my rambling consciousness ceases. The muddled and indulgent thoughts are burned away like morning mist. The pleasure of accusation and the pride of superiority have vanished. The unrelenting envy is gone. My mind is clear.

The Holy One waits, and the silence seems to repeat his question. Then I understand that I have no answer to give. The silence speaks for me too. All the pain, indignation, and perplexity have lost their substance. It is not that I fear to speak them or that I seek to hide them. They no longer exist. My inner conflict is over, and peace remains. No matter what the words, I see now that all my cries were but for him, and he is here. There is no question beyond his question and no answer beyond his presence. In the moment of my deliverance, I ponder the words of Nephi.

> And why should I yield to sin, because of my flesh?
> Yea, why should I give way to temptations, that the
> evil one have place in my heart to destroy my peace

75

and afflict my soul? Why am I angry because of
mine enemy?
Awake, my soul! No longer droop in sin. Rejoice, O my
heart, and give place no more for the enemy of
my soul.
Do not anger again because of mine enemies. Do not
slacken my strength because of mine afflictions.
Rejoice, O my heart, and cry unto the Lord, and say:
O Lord, I will praise thee forever; yea, my soul will
rejoice in thee, my God, and the rock of my
salvation.
(2 Nephi 4:27–30.)

The divine wisdom often teaches me, like Job, with
a question. Too often my questions are poorly put; they
harbor falsehoods among their presuppositions. To answer them would be to confirm these falsehoods. To ask
a question is easy, but to ask the right question, the true
question, that is something only God can do. His questions teach me to find my way, my truth, and my life in
him. They teach me patience and respect for learning
that is long and deep. My seed of faith must work in the
darkness of the soil before it finally reaches the light of
the sun. The plant must strive among the elements before it yields its blossoms. My answers must be my
blossoms made by the strength of my soul and the love
of God.

Time will tell. Someday I will look back and time
will mirror me to myself. What will I see? What will I
say? "I wasted time, and now doth time waste me"?
Modern clocks mislead with their endless circles of
time. Better to have an hourglass and to watch the
grains of sand slowly slipping away. Time is the stuff of

life. No one knows how much he has. No one can save any for the future.

To use time well I must cherish its worth and understand its nature. I must remember that each moment is a gift and that each moment is new. Not I but memories grow old. My challenge is to improve my time. (See Alma 34:33.) Time is God's gift to me; holiness is my gift to him. I am to make my life holy. As I improve myself, as my present is better than my past, God has promised to judge the whole of my life by reference to its latest result.

> If the wicked will turn from all his sins that he
> hath committed, and keep all my statutes, and do that
> which is lawful and right, he shall surely live, he shall
> not die.
> All his transgressions that he hath committed,
> they shall not be mentioned unto him: in his righ-
> teousness that he hath done he shall live.
> (Ezekiel 18:21–22.)

With the gift of time I can add my efforts to help renew the world. Instead of letting my moments fall into the past like raindrops into the sea, I can gather them into streams of mercy. My work is to cultivate the world with time, to create gardens in deserts. I must replace wildness with order, whim with discipline, passion with restraint, hatred with love.

In the account of creation I learn that time can be holy; the first thing that the Lord blessed and sanctified was time: the seventh day. The Sabbath is man's reminder of the purpose of life. The work of creation described in Genesis proceeds by means of division. Heaven is divided from earth, light from darkness, water ftom land, and so on. In the first six days the divisions are made in the spatial or physical world. Then at the end of creation another division is made, not in space but in time. The sacred comes into being in the world of time. The seventh day is holy, and it becomes man's first recurring token of holiness in his life. To remember the Sabbath day and to keep it holy is to renew the holy among men.

"Wherein have I wearied thee?" There is no weariness in the Lord's presence. Only when I wander away from him do burdens seem heavy. The law of the Lord is wisdom, and his wisdom is strength. Those who receive it "shall run and not be weary, and shall walk and not faint." (Doctrine and Covenants 89:20.) His teaching leads through time and into eternity. And there for him all moments are beginnings. "As one earth shall pass away, and the heavens thereof even so shall another come; and there is no end to my works." (Moses 1:38.) To those who fulfill the plan of development that he has given, the Lord promises the gift of eternal progression: the right and the power, the desire and the privilege, always to begin.

Beginnings are hard for me now. But each one prepares for the next and bestows its own measure of learning. Whatever I must do at the present moment, honest effort and prayer can bring forth goodness, even if I do not know how. Could Joseph have known, as he was carried off into slavery, what he knew years later? "Now therefore be not grieved, nor angry with yourselves, that ye sold me hither: for God did send me before you to preserve life." (Genesis 45:5.) During those years of servitude Joseph knew only that he must be faithful. He began in the house of Potiphar. Thrust down again by the evil deeds of others, he began again in prison. Over and over he began. And finally when famine sent his brothers to Egypt for food, it was from little Joseph, now second in authority only to Pharaoh, that they received it. From all Joseph's beginnings God fashioned the means to preserve the house of Jacob.

Who can know what lies hidden in a beginning? I can count the seeds in an apple, but can I count the apples in a seed? Every beginning is a seed, a hope, a dream. May mine ever bring forth good fruit.

8

Is Not the Life More Than Meat?

A child watched her mother polishing the silver candlesticks. "Why do you polish them so much?" she asked. "If I don't, they will grow dark and gray with tarnish." "What is tarnish?" "It is a stain, and I think it comes to remind us that our belongings are not beautiful by themselves. They shine only when they show our care." "Does everything tarnish?" "Yes, everything will tarnish, even though we can't always see it. When I polish my silver it reminds me that beauty comes not from what we have but from what we do with what we have. You see, we have to polish everything, even ourselves, to keep tarnish away."

It is common to hear praised the high standard of living in the United States, so common that I rarely pause to consider the words. What is meant by standard of living? What is a high standard of living? Suppose that a saint from ages past were to visit my time. Suppose I told him that my civilization had the highest standard of living in the history of the world. How would he understand the words? What would they lead him to expect? Could I imagine his face as I told him of home appliances, automobiles, airplanes, and computers? As we visited factories, looked at synthetic fibers and fertilizers, walked through fields of grain and dairy farms, would he be impressed or impatient? Would he wonder if I knew the meaning of my words? So accustomed am I to using them to refer to material things, I may forget that a standard of living can mean something else. I may forget the comment of a Hindu about the failure of Christian missionaries to make many converts in India. According to him all the Christian missionaries had one common failing: they lived too well; their standard of living belied their work. They took such care of themselves materially that it was impossible for the Hindus to take them in earnest spiritually. The Indians could not believe that such people were serious about holiness. As I think about it, all the great religions of the world were born under material conditions closer to India's than to America's.

If no civilization has been more fortunate materially than mine, then none has needed more to ponder the Lord's question, "Is not the life more than meat, and the body than raiment?" (Matthew 6:25.) Today I am told that you are what you eat and what you wear. I fear that my visitor from the past would feel disappointed with what is called the modern standard of living. He would wonder how a nominally Christian nation could have come so far from the teachings of Christ. He would think that no one appears to take Christ seriously enough. Everyone competes to improve his standard of living without having the slightest idea of what such a standard really means.

Material abundance is not the purpose of life. This does not mean, as some have supposed, that the things of the earth are evil, for God has pronounced them good. The question is only whether man is wise enough to use them as God intended.

> Yea, all things which come of the earth, in the season thereof, are made for the benefit and the use of man, both to please the eye and to gladden the heart;
> Yea, for food and for raiment, for taste and for smell, to strengthen the body and to enliven the soul.

And it pleaseth God that he hath given all these
things unto man; for unto this end were they made to
be used, with judgment, not to excess, neither by
extortion.

(Doctrine and Covenants 59:18–20.)

These few words provide a pattern for man's use of
nature. They make it clear that man's environment was
intended to support him but not to preoccupy him. Man's
task is to shape and mold what he needs—no more—for
the sake of righteous purposes, remembering that his
standard of living comes from heaven: "Ye shall be holy:
for I the Lord your God am holy." (Leviticus 19:2.) This
is the single standard for all ages, measuring every people.
How superior with reference to it is modern civilization?
How many modern gadgets and products were made
for the glory of God? What is the purport of a recent
history of civilization that calls the twentieth century
"heroic materialism"? Can man really enrich his life with
the things that are Caesar's? (See Luke 20:25). Can man
serve mammon for the sake of heaven? (Matthew 6:24).

Scripture records that material success is sometimes
one of the blessings bestowed upon the righteous. But it
also records that such success is a more dubious heritage
than the righteousness that produced it. How many civilizations have been able to survive their own material
success? Every people must face the haunting question
whether the achievements of the first generations deny
to the children the labor that made their parents strong.
For the parents nothing was to be had except as the
result of faith and work. But for the children this is not
so. For them the wells are already dug, the vineyards

planted, the houses built. For them the question will always be, what of all that they have received is of greatest worth? Could they "leave the land of their inheritance, and their gold, and their silver, and their precious things"? (1 Nephi 2:11.) Have the children still the power to become in some new way pioneers themselves? No question should be pondered more deeply by every parent. The needs of the body can be nursed into the pride of the flesh. Men can become unable to tell a want from a need. There are forces in this civilization that for their own profit try to create wants and keep the desire for material things at fever pitch. Always they have something new to offer. They seek to maintain in people a continual state of discontent and utter inability to be happy. They undermine respect for the virtues of self-denial and thoughtful restraint. Blotting out the past and concealing the future—what will happen after twenty years of alcohol, tobacco, drugs?—they focus all attention on the present moment and its craving for some immediate pleasure. The animals are protected from slavery to their present appetites by instinct. You never see a fat cat in the wild. But man is not governed by instinct; he was given free will. For protection from his own appetites man must turn to the larger context of choice; he must turn to time. A reflective awareness of the lessons of the past and the hopes of the future must guide man through the present.

Man learns through a heritage from the past that life is more than meat, more than a moment's gratification. Tradition links man to the spiritual wisdom of his forebears. Because tradition is so important for spiritual stability, evil always attempts to destroy it. The devil is a clever strategist; he isolates his victim if he can. What sins have followed those lured to lonely places who in the moment of temptation forgot the teachings of parents, of loved ones, of friends? And what doubts have troubled the minds of those who listened too long to words like these: "Behold, these things which ye call prophecies, which ye say are handed down by holy prophets, behold, they are foolish traditions of your fathers"? (Alma 30:14.)

Every child born into the world finds her place through the past, and it has been the duty of parents from the beginning to make that past clear. If the past and its meaning are blurred or uncertain, if the child has no sense of belonging to a live tradition, she will stumble and fall. To bestow a tradition parents must begin with themselves. They embody what they will teach for good or for evil. In the words of Rabbi Abraham Joshua Heschel, "To my child, I am either the embodiment of the spirit or its caricature. No book, no image, no symbol can replace my role in the imagination and the recesses of my child's soul."

On the minds of the young nothing is more indelible than the imprint of those they know and love. Nothing is dearer than the stories of Grandfather's youth or the tales of Grandmother's childhood. In the same way young imaginations are fed by visions of what their parents did when they were young, for in these simple things values and commitments are embedded. It is not a matter of transmitting information but of passing to the eye and heart of youth the flame of faith. Tradition is more than the lives and values of bodily ancestors. It includes the sacred stories of faith. A child descends not only from her parents but also from the covenant. Her heritage includes prophets and apostles, saints and martyrs, holy men and women whose lives bore witness of God. Testimonies of the past are an ensign for the future. A green grove in springtime, gold shining in the sun after fourteen hundred years in darkness, resurrected hands resting on the heads of two young men, angels singing from the temple's roof, shots and smoke in an infamous jail, the view of the sky from a covered wagon—these are the strands of tradition that bind each new generation to the covenant of the past.

How far from his youth was Enos when he went to "hunt beasts in the forests"? The record does not say. But while he was there, the teachings he had heard many times touched him for the first time. "The words which I had often heard my father speak concerning eternal life, and the joy of the saints, sunk deep into my heart. And my soul hungered." (Enos 1:3–4.) While searching for meat he learned that life is more than meat. The hunger of his soul overcame the hunger of his body because of the words of his father. How many times had they been repeated?

For every man the moment comes when all at once the time is at hand, and he must choose not only for today but for all his tomorrows. As he faces that moment, the very heavens watch and wait, hoping that the testimonies have been sufficient and that he like Enos will choose the Lord. Every word of witness that the faithful speak is a word of hope for someone's time of choosing.

Words, of course, are not enough alone. They must be supported by order and constant ways, by routine and by custom. Who can fathom what things are learned by children on bended knee long before the words they hear have meaning? In family rituals of worship and service, work and play, both body and mind obey. By familiar patterns renewed each day families bind upon themselves the promises first made in the past. Like silver, memories and covenants gleam with constant care. Patterns of behavior lay the basis for character. I learn to be good by being good and in no other way. Goodness must be a matter of habit long before it becomes a matter of thought. As Aristotle said, "It makes no small difference, then, whether we form habits of one kind or another from our very youth; it makes a very great difference, or rather all the difference."

A few years ago in the midst of campus riots a faithful worshiper, a professor, wended his way to services. He was confronted by a skeptical colleague. "Why do you go each week? You know everything will be the same." "Yes," replied the professor, "that is why I go, because everything will be the same." In the present age nothing seems to receive more praise than change and progress. But progress has no meaning unless it is measured by a constant standard. Nothing can progress unless something stays the same. In the whirlwind of change the rock of revealed tradition stands firm, and though all else should be blown away, it will not be moved. To those who will hear, its Maker speaks: "Fear not, little flock; do good; let earth and hell combine against you, for if ye are built upon my rock, they cannot prevail. . . . Look unto me in every thought; doubt not, fear not." (Doctrine and Covenants 6:34, 36.)

I am given the past; the future I must create. But all the work I perform can be done only in the present. Such is the paradox of human experience. In thought I may survey what has gone before and anticipate what will yet occur, but I can act only in the present moment. The commandments direct me toward my future. "Thou shalt . . ." is their call. They remind me that I live in the world of time. Righteousness is never accidental and never final. It must be chosen and renewed every moment.

A covenant is a promise made in the present with an eye to the future. And from the moment it is made, a covenant also becomes part of the past. It is there to remind me that I made it. The power to make and keep such promises binds man to heaven, for a covenant is a promise made to God.

Three things are needed to achieve goodness: God, his teaching, and a covenant. Without God my life has no enduring center; without his teaching it has no direction; without a covenant it has no commitment. The Bible tells that Potiphar's wife tempted Joseph "day by day." I can imagine her efforts—a prototype of all temptation—which were contrived to slowly wear him down. I can imagine that to him, a slave in a strange land, far from home and family, her attention might have been flattering. As the days went by, it might have become enticing. Perhaps in the moment of crisis the future seemed empty and the past a distant dream. Perhaps almost everything else faded before an intense desire

and the beckoning voice that called him. Almost everything. On the brink of sin Joseph cried out, "How . . .
can I do this great wickedness, and sin against God?"
(Genesis 39:9.)

Joseph was a son of the covenant. Even if discouragement brought him to a point at which he no longer cared
about himself, no longer had any concern for his actions,
his covenant remained. He was not his own. There was
God who cared, God who had concern. He was waiting,
watching, hoping that Joseph would be faithful. Joseph
was. By the power of his covenant with God he resisted
temptation. He rejected in a decisive moment one future
for another. Standing in the present, he steadied his balance and his resolve by grasping the immovable structure
that he had built long ago. With steel man can make a
bridge in space between two points. With a covenant he
can build a bridge in time spanning the past and present
and future to all eternity. Those who face every decision
with a conditional response, those who always withhold
irrevocable commitment in order to see how things work
out, deny themselves the power of goodness. Man was
not given freedom in order to be forever considering and
reconsidering. He was given it to learn fidelity to righteousness. I can never know in advance which act will
make all the difference for my future. I can only make my
covenants and suppose that everything will depend on
the moment at hand. As I do, at least once I will be right,
and that is enough.

9

Will Ye Also
Go Away?

All living beings have needs. From their environment they must draw their lives through such processes as eating, drinking, breathing. Man must do the same but with this difference: his needs are not only physical but social and spiritual.

I suppose that some animal might exist from the moment of its birth in isolation from others of its kind. Under favorable circumstances it would probably be able to maintain itself. It would do so by instinct. In contrast I cannot imagine that a child separated at birth from all human relationships would be able to grow up like a human being. If he survived physically, something would still be lost or left undeveloped. Human beings do not develop merely by instinct. As they are social beings, they can reach their potential or real nature only by teaching, by companionship, and by love.

From the moment that a child enters the world, the awareness that he has of being more than just a creature depends on others. His sense of being a person must be given to him by his interactions with those around him. He will come to know that he has worth through the care and recognition that he receives from other persons. By means of their respect for him he will gain self-respect.

By others the child is recognized, that is to say, taken seriously, acknowledged, accepted. His presence in the world makes a difference to them. Something is granted to him, and in turn something is expected from him. Recognition does not always imply approval. A child knows that he is recognized even as his parents reprove him, if they reprove him with love. A child who is never reproved may be a child who is neither recognized nor loved. He may be ignored, or he may be treated not like a person but like a tool or a toy.

The most important aspect of recognition is that it operates in two directions at once. A child learns that he can be fully recognized by others only as he is willing to recognize them in return. Mutual recognition creates all social relations. When an adult speaks to him, the child must listen. When the child speaks, the adult must listen. One gives and the other receives; but in a secondary sense, the first receives and the second gives at the same time. The adult gives advice; the child receives it. Yet equally, the listening child gives attention, and the speaking adult receives it. Both give and both receive at once. Unless these two overlapping actions occur, communication fails.

Although giving and receiving, recognizing and being recognized, are bound together, one is fundamental. Giving precedes receiving. Parents give to children in countless ways before children learn to be active receivers. At first a child receives only passively, which means that he really does not receive at all. In time he learns to receive actively. He smiles or laughs, and as he sees how this act is received in turn, he enters the social world of mutual recognition. In being given recognition with love he has learned to receive with love, and his act of receiving becomes his first act of giving. Man is a social being, but he is also a spiritual being. His spiritual capacity too must be nourished by the process of recognition. "God is love," and "we love him, because he first loved us." (1 John 4:16, 19.) Man is God's own child, loved and nurtured in more ways than he can know. But how often does man receive God's love passively, returning no smile nor laughter, offering no recognition of the Giver? As man remains passive before God, man's spirit weakens. God's purpose is to share himself with his children so that they can develop the active power to receive and to give spiritual gifts. "For unto him that receiveth it shall be given more abundantly, even power." (Doctrine and Covenants 71:6.) The Father wants his children to recognize him and to become his companions and friends, finally sharing with him all that he has.

To bring his children to him God has given prophets and revelations and blessings. At last he gave his Son to teach men how to give and receive with love. The coming of Christ into the world brought man the chance to learn how to become the friend of God. But from the start the Father's greatest gift found few who would receive it. "He came unto his own, and his own received him not." (John 1:11.) There were some who did receive Jesus and who followed his footsteps. They became his disciples, and he shared with them his message. The Master and his little band, these happy few, walked together bound by a love beyond telling. Yet along the road they took, something happened, and friends united fell apart. It was the message. "This is an hard saying; who can hear it?" (John 6:60.) For reasons that are not fully clear, the Lord's teaching offended some disciples. If only they would have faith, if only they would trust, in the end they would come to understand and accept his words. For now they must know that his teaching cannot follow their ideas. Had they not been through enough together to know that their Lord's wisdom had heaven as its source? It was no use.

> From that time many of his disciples went back, and walked no more with him.
> Then said Jesus unto the twelve, Will ye also go away?
>
> (John 6:66–67.)

Even the Lord can be abandoned as friends walk away. He too can be left alone, not understood. Those who speak of losing their faith do not speak accurately. It is he whom they have lost, he whom they have left. If he were only an idea or a doctrine, it would not matter so much. An idea can have no companions; it cannot be left alone. A doctrine cannot give or love; neither can it receive. But the Lord can; he can watch man turn and leave him. How many times has he watched? How many times has he been left alone?

The Lord seeks man even when man no longer seeks him. "O Jerusalem, Jerusalem, . . . how often would I have gathered thy children together, even as a hen gathereth her chickens under her wings, and ye would not!" (Matthew 23:37.) Although man often neglects to remember it, what man wants most only God can give. And what God wants most only man can give. God always seeks to give and longs to receive, but man fails to give and forgets to receive.

> And it came to pass that the God of heaven looked upon the residue of the people, and he wept; and Enoch bore record of it, saying: How is it that

the heavens weep, and shed forth their tears as the
rain upon the mountains?
    And Enoch said unto the Lord: How is it that
thou canst weep, seeing thou art holy, and from all
eternity to all eternity? . . .
    And thou has taken Zion to thine own bosom,
from all thy creations, from all eternity to all eternity;
and naught but peace, justice, and truth is the habita-
tion of thy throne; and mercy shall go before thy face
and have no end; how is it thou canst weep?
    The Lord said unto Enoch: Behold these thy
brethren; they are the workmanship of mine own
hands, and I gave unto them their knowledge, in the
day I created them; and in the Garden of Eden, gave
I unto man his agency;
    And unto thy brethren have I said, and also given
commandment, that they should love one another,
and that they should choose me, their Father; but behold, they are without affection.

(Moses 7:28–29, 31–33.)

Because man cannot always see or touch him, how
quickly he leaves the Lord. How slowly does he seek the
Lord. A grandfather was once interrupted by his young
grandson, who burst into the room sobbing. "Why are
you crying, my child?" "Oh, Grandfather, I was playing
hide-and-seek with my friend. I found such a good hiding place and waited. I waited for a long time, but
I couldn't hear him. I called, but he was gone. He hadn't
even tried to find me! He didn't look for me at all!" Upon
hearing this, the grandfather himself began to weep.
"My child," he said, "it is this way with God. He hides,
and no one will look for him."

If the Lord hides, it is only that I may seek and find him, only that my freedom will not be overwhelmed by his presence. He hides his hand that I may learn to walk, his face that I may listen for his voice. He withholds his blessing that I may give mine. "Verily thou art a God that hidest thyself, O God of Israel, the Saviour." (Isaiah 45:15.)

Some who turn from the Lord and his friendship feel justified. They say, if God can do this or allow that, then he does not exist or is not worthy of worship. Such a statement is arrogant. The arrogance does not lie in the fact that a man permits himself to challenge God; it lies in the man's unwillingness to wait for an answer. He has decided already that God cannot answer, and so he turns away impatiently, attributing to himself a concern that he feels God lacks.

To those who know the scriptures it is strange that any man should judge the world and find God lacking or that any man should think that his problem is new. What dilemma of human experience, what sorrow or suffering, what doubt or despair cannot be found in scripture? It is all there. Scripture is not just an answer book for the simple. Scripture contains all the questions too. Who is ready to trade questions with Job? Who can teach Jeremiah how to weep? What nation will choose to suffer with Israel? The Lord invites man to challenge him. "Testify against me," he says. (Micah 6:3.) God knows that man's righteous concerns are reflections of his own. As man is grieved by injustice, as man is oppressed by suffering, he shows the spark of divinity within him. Man learns his serious questions from God.

If anyone should doubt this, he may turn to those who question God most relentlessly. Who are they? Not the skeptics but the prophets. God's keenest questioners are his closest friends.

> And the men turned their faces from thence, and went toward Sodom: but Abraham stood yet before the Lord.
> And Abraham drew near, and said, Wilt thou also destroy the righteous with the wicked?. . . .
> Shall not the Judge of all the earth do right?
> (Genesis 18:22–23, 25.)

> Righteous art thou, O Lord, when I plead with thee: yet let me talk with thee of thy judgments: Wherefore doth the way of the wicked prosper? wherefore are all they happy that deal very treacherously?
> (Jeremiah 12:1.)

> O God, where art thou? And where is the pavilion that covereth thy hiding place?
> How long shall thy hand be stayed, and thine eye, yea thy pure eye, behold from the eternal heavens the wrongs of thy people and of thy servants, and thine ear be penetrated with their cries?
> Yea, O Lord, how long shall they suffer these wrongs and unlawful oppressions, before thine heart shall be softened toward them, and thy bowels be moved with compassion toward them?
> (Doctrine and Covenants 121:1–3.)

Whether the prophets plead for mercy or justice, their words before the Lord teach man what it means to be faithful. The prophets do not turn and walk away muttering their complaints. They stand and address the Lord. They stand for his children yet by him. There and only there can they find consolation and truth. The faithfulness of the prophets is their unshaken confidence that God can answer and will answer. "Surely I would speak to the Almighty, and I desire to reason with God. . . . Though he slay me, yet will I trust in him." (Job 13:3, 15.) Unlike those with weaker faith and greater pride, the prophets persist in their effort to know and understand God's will. Because he is good, they praise him; because he is kind, they approach him; because he is wise, they trust him.

Not only do the prophets question the Lord, they sometimes advise him as well.

> They made a calf in Horeb, and worshipped the molten image. . . .
> They forgat God their saviour, which had done great things in Egypt; . . .
> Therefore he said that he would destroy them, had not Moses his chosen stood before him in the breach, to turn away his wrath, lest he should destroy them.
> (Psalm 106:19, 21, 23.)

Moses "stood before him in the breach" and pleaded for mercy on behalf of the children of Israel. What can such a thing mean? Does the God of Israel need man "to turn away his wrath"? No, God does not need human advice. But man needs to learn humility, so God accepts counsel from him. If the Creator himself is willing to listen to his friends the prophets, how much more should man? As God hearkens to counsel, so should man. As God is not arbitrary and dictatorial, so man should not be. As God listens to pleas on behalf of the guilty, man cannot do less. "I will give unto you a pattern in all things, that ye may not be deceived." (Doctrine and Covenants 52:14.)

The pattern is clear. No one can afford to reject counsel; no one can be wise enough never to need it. Solitary judgment needs support from others. "Come now, and let us reason together, saith the Lord." (Isaiah 1:18.) Is it possible for man, so fond of office and distinction, so proud of authority and power, to grasp the meaning of these words? Can man understand the divine humility that offers to reason with him? God listens to all man's words. He hears the child with his wonder, the mother with her worry, the student with her doubts, the reformer with his demands. He hears all, he answers all, but "in his own time, and in his own way, and according to his own will." (Doctrine and Covenants 88:68.)

If he always receives my questions, sometimes he gives them back for me to keep and carry a little longer. These questions returned can teach me what answers could not, patience and fidelity. They can teach me the difference between dogma and faith. The Lord will let me bear them until I have learned what he intends. For now all questions, however hard, reduce finally to one.

How shall I answer when the time and the task seem long, when persuasive voices urge me to follow them— how shall I answer those mild eyes and quiet words, "Will ye also go away?"

10

Whom Seekest Thou?

Among all the creatures on earth, only man seems unable to be content. Wingless, man would fly; weaponless, he would conquer; mortal, he would escape death. By his own art man has made highways in the sky and has obtained dominion over all of nature. But nature still claims the last victory. Man will die. In a thousand stories and legends the dream persists that this need not be so, but nature's reckoning remains unchanged. Though mankind may continue, individual men fulfill their days and depart.

In every age there have been those who taught that death is not defeat. Plato taught that true lovers of wisdom "make dying their profession, and . . . to them of all men death is least alarming." At the center of this view was the conviction that the world of nature in which man lives, with all its change and transformation, is just a shadowy image of eternal reality. The body, the senses, space and time—these are illusions from which death removes man. By reason alone does man become aware of the true and rational reality, and by death alone does he achieve it. Until the moment of his death man lingers in the present world catching occasional mental glimpses of the realm of true being, the realm to which his thoughts alone can rise while he lives.

> Life, like a dome of many-coloured glass,
> Stains the white radiance of Eternity,
> Until Death tramples it to fragments. —Die,
> If thou wouldst be with that which thou dost seek!

Like Plato, the poet Shelley offered in these lines solace for death in a realm beyond death. But the eternal realm that they spoke of provides no continuation of life as I know it but something different altogether. "But is an eternal and endless life after death," asked Spanish philosopher Miguel de Unamuno, "indeed thinkable? How can we conceive the life of a disembodied spirit? . . . The immortality of the pure soul, without some sort of body or spirit covering, is not true immortality." To leave everything earthly behind is to leave life itself behind. For one who grieves over eyes now closed and a voice now stilled, there is no consolation in the thought of a disembodied, impersonal eternity beyond the grave. A purely rational reality is not enough. Man's joys and loves and times of beauty and goodness are all bound up with the tangibility of flesh and earth, the motion of wind and breath, the sound of laughter and song. Man knows what life is. He wants nothing less, nothing else.

It is clear enough that the cycle of nature requires both birth and death. It is clear that death provides an end and thus a structure to every life. Because man has only a little time, he learns that it is precious and that life is urgent. In a world where all things grow old, death is a merciful conclusion to the infirmities of age. All these things may be admitted. What cannot be admitted is that death shall be the final end. The words that speak of eternal sleep only remind man that the sleep he knows always ends in waking. And so he asks, "If a man die, shall he live again?" (Job 14:14.)

Though I may first utter this question in grief over the loss of a loved one, its significance is deeper than my grief. It is not simply a yes that I seek. I want to know the meaning of life itself. Why is there life? Why is there death? What purpose is served by all the bliss and sorrow that man is heir to? There will always be those who say there is no purpose. But even if I could not refute this view, neither could I accept it. The statement that there is no purpose only calls forth my question again. Why is there no purpose? I cannot think or talk or live except in terms of purpose.

Throughout world literature the answers of the ages to these questions are recorded. In the traditions of the various peoples may be found the wisdom of those who have pondered man's condition. In their teachings many insights recur and many themes are common. Compassion and love mingle together, revealing the common humanity that must face a common problem. Still the traditions are not all the same. Among them is one that utters a claim different from all the others, a claim so overwhelming that once it is heard, no other can ever equal its power, even before it is believed. "God himself shall come down among the children of men, and shall redeem his people." (Mosiah 15:1.)

In its fullness the story of man's redemption is the history of the world, and each person who has ever lived plays his role. But the divine wisdom has given the heart of the story in scripture, so that man may ponder it always. The meaning of this story may be viewed in three gardens and three questions, in the evening, in the night, and in the dawn.

God planted a garden eastward in Eden and placed there the parents of the human family. It was a garden of paradise, untouched by sorrow, sin, or death. How long Adam and Eve dwelt there cannot be told. Of their activities the record is mostly silent. They were alone. No children's games amused their eyes. Only the beauties of nature surrounded them. Such beauty though marvelous was not enough. God knew it was not. With the gift of life he wished also to bestow the gift of choice, the power to grow and to begin. The unfathomable paradox of love is that the greatest gift could not be given. God could prepare the way, but man would have to step forward by himself, for the gift was freedom.

Every beginning is also an ending. What was yields its place to that which is to come. Man's beginning could occur only by means of a choice that man himself had made, a choice that would require leaving something behind. God provided for that choice when he planted the tree of knowledge of good and evil. He forbade the eating of its fruit and told Adam and Eve the consequence of eating it. "Thou shalt not eat of it: for in the day that thou eatest thereof thou shalt surely die." (Genesis 2:17.)

But the Lord did not simply say that eating the fruit was forbidden. He said that eating it would bring death and added, "Nevertheless, thou mayest choose for thyself, for it is given unto thee." (Moses 3:17.) Adam and Eve were given the right to choose for themselves on the condition that they would die if the fruit were eaten. No one who lives on the other side of their momentous choice can pretend to grasp the deliberations of their hearts as they made the decision to choose knowledge. Somehow in the wisdom of their innocence they reached beyond it, and in choosing knowledge and death they chose life for all.

If Adam had not transgressed he would not have
fallen, but he would have remained in the garden
of Eden. And all things which were created must
have remained in the same state in which they were
after they were created; and they must have remained
forever, and had no end.

And they would have had no children; wherefore
they would have remained in a state of innocence,
having no joy, for they knew no misery; doing no
good, for they knew no sin.

But behold, all things have been done in the wisdom of him who knoweth all things.

Adam fell that men might be; and men are, that
they might have joy.

(2 Nephi 2:22–25.)

In the fall of Adam man was born. At the end of
Eden the beginning of a long journey was made. Man
would leave the first garden never to return. Sometime
after the forbidden fruit had been eaten, Adam and Eve
heard the Lord "walking in the garden in the cool of
the day." (Genesis 3:8.) Somewhere in the garden that
evening the parents of humanity heard for the first time
the Lord's question, "Where art thou?" It was a question
that they and their children after them would hear again
throughout their lives, calling, guiding, along all the
paths ahead. The Lord's voice would be their strength.

The mortal pilgrimage began. No longer was man
blessed with the personal presence of God. By faith
man was to walk. No longer sheltered in the garden,
he found his way in a world that could be hostile, for
everywhere was the influence of the adversary. There
were moments of beauty, of love and companionship, of

triumph over obstacles. But above all these like a dark cloud rested the consequence of man's first choice. The story of man's life was a story in which everything would soon perish. Time would finally take away all that was dear. Man, a little lower than the angels, knew that at the end of all his triumphs and hopes was an open grave and a few spadefuls of earth.

Man's ideals never seemed quite within his grasp. Always he encountered a dark and ominous force trying to pull him down, tempting him with unholy thoughts and deeds. In the midst of his anguish he sometimes cried out with weariness and grief.

> I have seen all the works that are done under the sun; and, behold, all is vanity and vexation of spirit.
> That which is crooked cannot be made straight: and that which is wanting cannot be numbered.
> (Ecclesiastes 1:14–15.)

But beside this voice there was another voice, the voice of a small, politically unimportant people claiming that beyond all hope and from beyond the world help would come. "For I know that my redeemer liveth, and that he shall stand at the latter day upon the earth." (Job 19:25.) Could such a thing be believed? In a tiny province of the Roman Empire an aged man called Simeon had believed all his life. And then he knew beyond doubt.

> And, behold, there was a man in Jerusalem, whose name was Simeon; and the same man was just and devout, waiting for the consolation of Israel: and the Holy Ghost was upon him.

And it was revealed unto him by the Holy Ghost, that he should not see death, before he had seen the Lord's Christ.

And he came by the Spirit into the temple: and when the parents brought in the child Jesus, to do for him after the custom of the law,

Then took he him up in his arms, and blessed God, and said,

Lord, now lettest thou thy servant depart in peace, according to thy word:

For mine eyes have seen thy salvation,

Which thou hast prepared before the face of all people.

(Luke 2:25–31.)

Who can know how soon the burden was laid upon young Jesus of Nazareth? He was raised by wise and good parents, and in the tradition of his people he was taught both a trade and the sacred scriptures. Already at the age of twelve he was about his Father's business. At the early time when the thoughts of children explore their unknown future, and they wonder what they will be, Jesus knew what he must be. He knew that he was the ransom for sin, "the Lamb slain from the foundation of the world." (Revelation 13:8.)

His life in its very nature was defined by his mission. There was no room for selfishness, no time for levity, no relief from responsibility. In the sublime solitude of his calling and perfection he walked among men, realizing as no one else before or since that every step he took marked a way that all mankind would follow. Not only his words but his life would be his teaching, and not only his life but his death. He knew that before him lay a battle with the prince of darkness. Long before that crisis came his face was set toward Jerusalem and a garden called Gethsemane. There all things would hang in balance.

It was night. With three disciples the Savior of the world went to meet his foe. As the duel began, his seconds fell asleep, worn out with grief. In terrible anguish he stepped off the brink of all human support and plummeted downward, grappling with his adversary in his duty of love. In a way unknown to man he plumbed the depths of sorrow for sin. Beyond comprehension he descended below all things, leaving nothing outside his redeeming power. And then he rose. With bloody sweat and trembling frame the Lord spoke, "Why sleep ye?" (Luke 22:46.) In the disciples' stead an angel had come from heaven to strengthen Jesus in his hour of need. (See Luke 22:43.) But why had they slept? Though men be good, men are weak, and in the extremities of life's trials, no man can ever count wholly on another. There is only one who will never fail. "My help cometh from the Lord," who "shall neither slumber nor sleep." (Psalm 121:2, 4.) Jesus had borne the world's weakness in a garden and a night. Now he must carry it up a hill toward day.

As he hung on the cross, he met that which was crucial to his final victory but almost too much to bear. "My God, my God, why hast thou forsaken me?" (Mark 15:34.) What led the Lord to quote this ancient prayer? (See Psalm 22:1.) The power of heaven seems at the last to have been withdrawn, so that he was left by himself. The awful contest was to be his alone to win or lose. From the purity and love of his own soul he drew his last measure of strength and fulfilled his quest. "It is finished," said the Redeemer of the world, and then he died. (John 19:30.) Even as the Lord's heart broke, so too did the power of evil over men, and "redeemed from the fall they have become free forever, knowing good from evil; to act for themselves and not to be acted upon." (2 Nephi 2:26.) And though in history some men might live and die never hearing the name of Christ, yet because he lived and died, they may hope to live again.

On the third day the friends of Christ came in the morning to the place of his burial. They found the grave empty and the stone rolled away. In confusion and grief all but Mary departed. Weeping by herself in the garden outside the tomb, perhaps she recalled the Lord's words, spoken not far from another tomb and not so long ago: "I am the resurrection, and the life: he that believeth in me, though he were dead, yet shall he live: And whosoever liveth and believeth in me shall never die." (John 11:25–26.) Then Mary heard a voice and a question: "Whom seekest thou?" (John 20:15.) Turning, she beheld the risen Christ walking again in the garden, not of the evening or the night, but of the dawn.

From that Easter morning until now the Lord's question to Mary reaches down the countless paths of every life to every heart. Blessed are they whose answer can be: Only thee, Lord, only thee.

Notes

1
Where Art Thou?

Page 3 "All men by nature . . ."
Aristotle, *Metaphysics*, Book 1, Chapter 1.

Pages 5–6 "He was good . . ."
Plato, *Timaeus*, 29d.

Page 8 Once a man named Zusia . . .
See Martin Buber, *Hasidism and Modern Man* (New York: Horizon Press, 1958), 140.

2
Do Not I Fill Heaven and Earth?

Page 16 "The world is charged with . . ."
Gerard Manley Hopkins, "God's Grandeur."

Page 18 "How will the serpent . . ."
Joseph Smith, *Teachings of the Prophet Joseph Smith* (Salt Lake City: Deseret Book, 1938), 71.

Pages 20–21 "Master of the Universe . . ."
See Samuel H. Dresner, *Levi Yitzhak of Berditchev* (New York: Hartmore House, 1974), 106.

Page 22 "first, fast, last friend."
Gerard Manley Hopkins, "The Lantern Out of Doors."

3
What Mean the Testimonies?

Pages 26–27 "When he read . . . "
Saint Augustine, *Confessions*, Book VI, Chapter 3.

Page 27 Plato expressed doubt . . .
Plato, *Phaedrus*, 27d.

Page 28 My language sets "the limits of my world."
Ludwig Wittgenstein, *Tractatus Logico-Philosophicus*, 5.6.

Page 31 "read, mark, learn, and inwardly digest."
The Book of Common Prayer, Second Sunday in Advent,
The Collect.

Page 34 "It was human testimony . . . "
Joseph Smith, *Lectures on Faith* (Salt Lake City: Deseret
Book, 1985), 2:56.

Page 34 ". . . neither joy, nor love, nor light . . . "
Matthew Arnold, "Dover Beach."

4
Whom Shall I Send?

Page 40 "Society cannot exist unless . . . "
Edmund Burke, *A Letter from Mr. Burke, to a Member of the
National Assembly* (New York, 1791).

Page 45 "Joy of the desolate . . . "
"Come, Ye Disconsolate," *Hymns* (Salt Lake City: The
Church of Jesus Christ of Latter-day Saints), 115.

NOTES

5
Fear Ye Not Me?

Page 50 "all things are full . . ."
Aristotle, *On the Soul*, Book I, Chapter 5.

Page 54 "Pull down thy vanity . . ."
Ezra Pound, *Cantos* (New York: New Direction, 1948), Canto LXXXI.

Page 55 "the natural and just object . . ."
Joseph Butler, *Fifteen Sermons upon Human Nature*, Preface.

Page 57 Can I who am a pilgrim . . .
See John Bunyan, *The Pilgrim's Progress*, the First Part.

7
Wherein Have I Wearied Thee?

Pages 72–73 "All things excellent . . ."
Benedict de Spinoza, *Ethics*, Part V, Proposition XLII.

Page 76 "I wasted time . . ."
William Shakespeare, *Richard II*, Act V, scene V.

8
Is Not the Life More Than Meat?

Pages 83–84 I may forget the comment . . .
See Thomas Merton, *The Seven Storey Mountain* (New York: Harcourt Brace, 1948), Part Two, i, iii.

Page 85 "heroic materialism."
Kenneth Clark, *Civilisation* (New York: Harper & Row, 1970), Chapter 13.

Page 87 "To my child . . ."
Abraham Joshua Heschel, *The Insecurity of Freedom* (New York: Schocken Books, 1972), 83.

Page 89 "It makes no small difference . . ."
Aristotle, *Nicomachean Ethics*, Book II, Chapter 1.

9
Will Ye Also Go Away?

Page 99 A grandfather was . . .
See Abraham Joshua Heschel, *Man Is Not Alone* (New York: Farrar, Straus & Young, 1951), 154.

10
Whom Seekest Thou?

Page 107 "make dying their profession . . ."
Plato, *Phaedo*, 67e.

Page 107 "Life, like a dome . . ."
Percy Bysche Shelley, "Adonais."

Page 108 "But is an eternal and endless life . . ."
Miguel de Unanmuno, *Tragic Sense of Life* (New York: Dover, 1954), 223–24, 233.

Old Testament

New Testament

Doctrine and Covenants

Pearl of Great Price

36156985R00080

Made in the USA
San Bernardino, CA
14 July 2016